HOW TO START A
BUSINESS WEBSITE

Other **21ST CENTURY ENTREPRENEUR** *Titles*
from Avon Books

The 21st Century
ENTREPRENEUR

HOW TO START A BUSINESS WEBSITE

MIKE POWERS

A Third Millennium Press Book

AVON BOOKS ▲ NEW YORK

AVON BOOKS, INC.
1350 Avenue of the Americas
New York, New York 10019

Copyright © 1999 by Third Millennium Press, Inc., Stephen M. Pollan, and Mike Powers
Cover illustration by Nick Gaetano
Published by arrangement with Third Millennium Press, Inc.
ISBN: 0-380-79713-5
www.avonbooks.com

Library of Congress Cataloging in Publication Data:

Powers, Mike.
  How to start a business website / Mike Powers.
      p.   cm. — (The 21st century entrepreneur)
  ''A Third Millennium Press book.''
  1. New business enterprises—Computer networks.   2. Business
enterprises—Computer networks.   3. Web sites.   I. Title.
II. Series.
HD62.5.H683   1999   99-24021
025.04'068—dc21   .   CIP

First Avon Books Trade Paperback Printing: October 1999

AVON TRADEMARK REG. U.S. PAT. OFF. AND IN OTHER COUNTRIES, MARCA REGISTRADA, HECHO
EN U.S.A.

Printed in the U.S.A.

OPM   10   9   8   7   6   5   4   3

CONTENTS

HOW TO START A BUSINESS WEBSITE

INTRODUCTION

WELCOME TO THE FUTURE

One winter day early in 1996, I walked into the future.

I was in the middle of writing a book on how to start a mail order business and had become interested in the growing number of businesses that were setting up shop on the World Wide Web. This was mail order with a new twist, I realized, and I wanted to learn more about it.

I didn't have to look far. I had for a number of months seen a small ad in the back of the free weekly newspaper in the town where I live—Ithaca, New York—for a business called Jim's Ithaca Music Shop. In addition to the name, the only other information the ad contained was a Web address: *http://www.jims.com/*. There was no street address or phone number. There were no business hours. There was nothing that one would normally expect to see in a business ad. I was intrigued.

When I logged on to the Web to see what Jim's Ithaca Music Shop was all about, the first thing I encountered was Dexter, a cartoon beatnik who serves as tour guide through the site and the various categories of compact discs Jim has for sale.

Dexter directs visitors to "The Hip List," Jim's esoteric selection of jazz, blues, rock, and folk recordings from the '50s to the '90s. He also shows the way to "The $8.00 List," Jim's selection of discounted closeouts. Other pointers take visitors to an order form and pages that describe the business and recent developments at Jim's. There was also some other important information—fax and phone numbers, an e-mail address, a street address, and Jim's last name, Spitznagel. As it turned out, he lives just a few blocks from my office. I contacted him the next day and made an appointment to interview him for the book.

When I went to visit Jim a week or so later, I was greeted by a tall man in his mid-forties with a neatly trimmed dark beard, small wire-framed glasses, and a gentle, congenial manner. He led me to his place of business, a large third-floor attic that covers his entire house. The attic had been finished with Sheetrock, painted a stark white, and had thick black wall-to-wall carpet. The walls were covered with photographs and other mementos of Jim's years as a record and compact disc retailer. His store, down the street from Carnegie-Mellon University in Pittsburgh, had been voted the best record store in the city five of the eighteen years he owned it. One wall had a large rack containing a stereo. Another wall was lined with shelves to hold the 4,000 or so CDs Jim keeps in stock. A long desk held a computer, fax machine, and printer, as well as piles of catalogs and phone books.

Over the next couple of hours Jim told me how he'd landed in cyberspace—how he'd sold his Pittsburgh business and ended up helping plan and then managing the gift shop and mail order business for the city's new Andy Warhol Museum. There, Jim received his baptism in doing business on the Web. He worked with a consultant to set up a Website for the shop, and the day the museum opened they received orders from Japan, Germany, and South America. He says it made a huge impression on him.

When marriage brought Jim to Ithaca, his initial plan was to start another storefront CD business. But the price of commercial leases and the prospect of another life of twelve-hour days quickly soured him on the idea and started him thinking about starting a Web business. He spent the next three months researching the Internet and studying other businesses on the Web.

On June 1, 1995, he turned on his computer and Jim's Ithaca Music Shop was up and running. Within just a few months he was sending CDs to customers around the world. In addition to just about every state in the U.S., he's filled orders from England, Finland, the Netherlands, South Africa, Japan, and Brazil. He has even gotten an order from China.

As I listened to Jim describe his business and looked around his attic office, I realized this was the perfect way to run a retail business. Every person in the world with access to the Web is a potential customer, I thought. Plus he had virtually no overhead. He didn't have to worry about shoplifters or vandalism. He didn't have to worry about lousy weather keeping customers away. And he was always open! He could be sleeping, having dinner with his family, running errands, seeing a movie, or even on vacation, *and still be selling merchandise! The orders keep rolling in!*

This book was inspired by that visit to Jim Spitznagel. In the two years since I met him, the Web has exploded, as its commercial potential has become more and more obvious. There are now tens of thousands of businesses with Websites, ranging from multinational corporate giants to folks like Jim, selling stuff out of their attics.

The presence of so many businesses online has raised a very important question that every business owner thinking about trying to do business on the Web must ask themselves—what's the rationale for me being in cyberspace in the first place?

One of the many interesting behaviors generated by the Web has been the blind scramble on the part of America's corporations to create their own sites. Exhibiting the lemminglike behavior that so often characterizes American business, they've rushed headlong into cyberspace for the simple reason that everyone else has done the same. It's only after investing hundreds of thousands of dollars in hardware, software, and Website design and maintenance costs that they stop, scratch their heads, and ask themselves, "Now what?" For companies that don't operate traditional retail businesses, the Web is basically just another very expensive form of advertising. Only time will tell whether the return on investment is worth it.

But for people selling goods—and to a lesser extent, services—the Web is a wonderful new environment in which to do business. Think of it as mail order without the cost of writing, designing, printing catalogs, and maintaining an 800 number. Or imagine a storefront that can be visited by every person in the world who has a computer and an Internet connection. Your electronic business can be patronized by customers with a few keystrokes. They can order merchandise with just a few more. Sure, there are costs, but they pale in comparison to the costs of running a traditional storefront or mail order business.

I've written this book for people like Jim Spitznagel—small business owners who want to explore either starting a business on the Web or expanding an existing business onto the Web. Although it discusses many technical issues, the book is more about the business of being online than the technology of the Web. And even though it's focused on small businesses, many of the points covered are applicable to businesses of all sizes.

The first chapter looks at the development of the Internet and World Wide Web. This remarkable technology has turned into what many people feel is the most important tool for communication since Gutenberg invented the printing press.

Chapter 2 examines the question we just discussed: Is the Web right for your business? Just because *it*'s there doesn't necessarily mean *you* need to be there, too.

Chapter 3 takes you on a brief tour of cyberspace and discusses the methods of navigation and communication in this brave new world.

No business, whether in the physical world or on the Web, can afford to open up shop without a firm business plan beneath it. Yet many online merchants fail for this very reason—lack of planning. Chapter 4 discusses how to create a business plan for your Web business and looks at some of the costs you'll face in setting up shop.

Chapter 5 will show you how to get "wired"—how to get your Internet connection, hire an Internet Service Provider, and obtain your domain name, or electronic "address." It also looks at the equipment you'll need to set up a Website—computers, modems, fax machines, printers, and the software needed to make them all work.

Chapter 6 shows you how to build your Website—what to look for in a Website designer, how to evaluate other sites, and the criteria for a good site.

From its earliest days, the growth of commerce on the Web has been slowed by the issue of security. Many people have been understandably reluctant to send out credit card numbers and other personal information over the Internet, and their concerns have kept them from patronizing Web businesses. But with so much money at stake, this problem has received a great deal of attention, and the problems, if they ever really existed in the first place, have largely been solved. We'll look at the issue of security on the Web in Chapter 7.

Once your online business is up and running, you'll have to confront the question I mentioned earlier: "Now what?" The Web is a huge, fairly disorganized place, and once you're there, one of your biggest challenges will be to let people *know* you're there. Chapter 8 looks at promoting your site, and the various services and strategies you can use to make sure your customers can find you.

Just as in a traditional storefront operation, you can't make a sale on the Web until the customer enters your store. So once potential customers find you and your Web address, you need to be able to entice them to visit. Chapter 9 will show you how to conduct marketing and advertising campaigns that will bring people through the door.

Your online business will share another important trait with conventional businesses—the responsibility to provide good customer service. No business can succeed without it. Chapter 10 discusses customer service and how to process orders and ship your merchandise.

Like any other business, a Web business is vulnerable to a host of problems, many of which can sink your digital ship. We'll examine some of the most common in Chapter 11.

In Chapter 12, we'll pay a return visit to Jim Spitznagel. His online business is more than three years old now, which makes him a grizzled veteran among Web merchants. We'll find out what he's learned and ask him what advice he'd give the budding electronic entrepreneur.

Finally, in Chapter 13, we'll take a look at some Websites you can learn from. They represent businesses of various sizes and descriptions from around the country. Some, like Amazon.com, are enormous, and others are closer in size to Jim Spitznagel's business. All of them have excellent site design, navigation features, and ordering procedures.

When you've finished this book, you'll have all the information you'll need to go into business on the Web. But your work will just be starting. As I mentioned before, things are changing faster than ever before in cyberspace. The only way to survive is to keep pace with new developments and use them to your advantage.

And be assured they will be to your advantage. There are billions of dollars to be made on the World Wide Web, both for the people who do business there and those who develop the technologies to make it all possible. Entrepreneurs the world over are hard at work developing new tools to bring you and your customers together. We're just seeing the tip of the iceberg. Happy reading, and good luck!

WHERE DID THIS THING COME FROM, ANYWAY?

Sometimes the best things happen almost by accident.

That's certainly the case with the Internet and the World Wide Web. There's a good chance that someday we may look back and consider them the happiest accidents in the history of the planet. In the last six or seven years they've changed the way we communicate more rapidly than any development in history.

At its most basic, this remarkable technology allows us to send messages to one another. Whether you work for a small company, a large corporation, a university, a government agency, or even have your own business in your home, there's a good chance that most of your day-to-day communication is now done electronically via e-mail. Type in a message, hit a button, and in an instant it's delivered to the computer of a friend or colleague around the corner or around the world.

And what's happened to your telephone? Well, if you're like me, you use it to call your mom, who, if she's like mine, hasn't even mastered the automated teller yet, let alone attempted to communicate in cyberspace.

But that's just the ground floor. On more sophisticated levels, the Internet and World Wide Web are electronic reference libraries, research data bases, books, art galleries, newspapers, magazines, literary salons, catalogs, stores, gambling parlors, and even village gathering places. The Web's ability to transmit images, sound, and other media give it almost unlimited potential, and people are dreaming up new uses for it almost every day. As amazing as things have been so far, they've only scratched the surface. It's sometimes hard to believe that most of this has only been around since 1994. The next ten to twenty years are going to be a lot of fun.

THE INTERNET VS. THE WORLD WIDE WEB

Before we go any further, we need to clear up something that confuses a lot of people. They hear Internet. They hear World Wide Web. Are these two the same thing, they wonder, or is there a difference?

The answer is they're both the same and different. The Internet is the global linkage of computer networks that allows information to be sent at breakneck speed around the world. The only catch is that the information that can be sent is limited to text. Think of it as the hardware for the whole endeavor.

The World Wide Web, on the other hand, is what most people think of when they talk about the Internet. This is because the Web is what finally attracted them into cyberspace. It has the ability to transfer not just text, but also images, video, and audio. When the technology began to catch on in 1993, it single-handedly turned the Internet from a medium that was largely the realm of researchers and academics—who were connected at work—and a relatively small contingent of computer geeks—who logged on from home—to a place where everyone can find something of interest. At that point, there were maybe two million people connected to the Web. Today there may be as many as forty million, and their numbers are growing exponentially. For people who plan on doing business there, every one of them is a potential customer.

HOW IT ALL STARTED

In a sense, we can thank the fears that gripped the nation during the Cold War for the creation of the Internet. It all started in the late 1950s, when the Department of Defense's Advanced Research Projects Agency launched a project called ARPANET.

The idea was to create a nationwide linkage of large (and, supposedly, immune from nuclear attack) mainframe computers to support military research projects. The users agreed to a standard operating protocol that allowed them to communicate with one another.

By the mid 1960s, the network had begun to expand. There were a lot of civilian institutions collaborating with the military on its projects, including a number of the country's biggest corporations and foremost research universities. Involved in their own research as well as working with the military, they realized the network was a wonderful tool for communicating, sharing data, and collaborating on projects. In the 1980s, the introduction of the personal computer and electronic workstation increased the demand for presence on the Internet even further. People were discovering the vast wealth of information that could be accessed over the giant network. Eventually, as more and more independent networks wanted to come online, overloading became a serious issue.

In 1985, to help solve the problem, the National Science Foundation established four super computing centers—at Cornell University (where I spend much of my time), the University of Pittsburgh, the University of Illinois, and the University of California at San Diego—linked by high-speed lines capable of carrying an extraordinary amount of data. Much like the airports in Atlanta and Chicago act as hubs for major airline routes, these four sites act as hubs for the trillions of bytes of electronic information that whiz around the country every second of every day.

In its earliest days, most Internet users were engineers, physicists, and other technical folks working on complicated projects. Data transmission was limited to text, and most communication centered on research and the sharing of data. Nothing real exciting happened, at least not in the popular culture sense. Gradually, though, as more people discovered the Internet, other uses popped up.

E-mail began to supplant the telephone as a convenient means of communication. More and more information became available on electronic data bases maintained by universities and corporations. People began gathering electronically in "chat rooms'' devoted to the discussion of virtually every topic imaginable. A person could (and still can) sit in his study and have an earnest discussion on Shakespeare, sitcoms, sex, or whatever else tickled his fancy with people he'd never met or even heard of. In fact, the anonymity of the Internet is what attracted a lot of its early recreational users. You might be a dweeb in real life, but in cyberspace you could be whoever you wanted to be, and no one was the wiser.

The Internet was a very exclusive place for quite a while because unless you knew what you were looking for, finding your way around was quite difficult. There was also a kind of purity to the whole endeavor. People knew they were part of something special, and there was a sense of community and selflessness. Users freely shared software with one another, and the idea that the Internet might be used for commercial purposes was viewed with horror.

Then Tim Berners-Lee came along.

In the late 1980s, the London-born software engineer (he has a degree in theoretical physics from Queen's College at the University of Oxford) was working for CERN, a particle physics laboratory in Switzerland. He wanted to create a system that would help electronically linked researchers work more constructively together. The results were hypertext markup language (HTML), hypertext transfer protocol (HTTP), and an early form of uniform resource locator (URL). Together, these three software programs form the foundation of the Web.

Berners-Lee put his new software on the Internet in 1991, but it would still be a couple of years before it really took off. The springboard was the first successful ''browser,'' a software program that lets users roam around the Web from one place to another and view images as well as text. The program was called Mosaic and was developed at the University of Illinois by a team of talented software engineers, including a young man named Marc Andreesen. (Today, Andreesen, one of the founders of the hugely popular Netscape, is worth millions.)

With images and an ever-increasing amount of information available—and the fact that, with just a modicum of technical expertise, anyone could create their own presence in cyberspace—this strange new world that was so foreign to so many for so long began to seem decidedly appealing. People quickly explored its potential, and it wasn't long before some of them began to make money. The first online merchants included companies like Prodigy and America Online, who started using the Web to provide services to customers who paid a monthly, use-based fee. But even then, their subscribers were limited to the companies' offerings. They didn't really enjoy complete access to the Web.

That has since changed. Today, the availability of even better browser programs, such as Netscape Navigator and, more recently, Microsoft Internet Explorer, has made finding your way around the Web easier than ever. Most people can obtain a direct Internet connection from a local provider for fifteen or twenty dollars a month. The competition has forced the commercial services to provide full access as well.

But these methods of connection are still quite slow and ungainly. If you've spent any time on the Web, you've experienced how painfully slow it can often be to move from one site to another. Heavy traffic sometimes makes it impossible to access a site altogether. As we'll see later in the chapter, there are better systems just over the horizon. It won't be long before they're here.

JUST HOW BIG IS THE WEB?

Nobody really knows, although the most reliable estimates of Internet users puts the number at somewhere between 57 and 70 million worldwide. Of those, anywhere from 30 to 40 million may have Web access. No one knows for sure because there's no way of monitoring the system. In a sense, the whole thing is kind of like a giant electronic cooperative—new networks join and agree to use the standard addressing protocol to send information.

How fast are businesses coming online? In early 1996, Inter-NIC, an organization that maintains Internet addresses, reported that as of December 8, 1995, there were 152,341 commercial Websites (sites whose electronic addresses contain .com, like llbean.com or landsend.com). It also reported there were 2,000 such sites being added each week. Around the same time, Yahoo, a popular site that collects and categorizes Websites of all descriptions, reported it was receiving 5,000 submissions a week for evaluation and inclusion in its lists.

WHO RUNS IT?

No one "runs" the Internet or the Web. That would be impossible. But it does have a management of sorts, a group called the Internet Society. It's made up of volunteers who promote global information exchange and establish operating standards. A subgroup, the Internet Architecture Board, acts as a steering committee on addressing protocols and other issues.

Another "management" organization is run by Berners-Lee, who's now at the Massachusetts Institute of Technology. His group is called the World Wide Web Consortium, or W3C, and has staff people located around the world and more than 200 member organizations, including many of the biggest names in the communications and computer industries. The W3C's mission is to preserve the integrity of the Web and make sure its countless pieces remain linked as one global network. Each member firm in the W3C signs a contract giving Berners-Lee the final sign-off on Web specifications. He and his group will probably have more to say about how the Web evolves than any other entity.

SO WHERE IS ALL THIS HEADED?

What we've seen so far—both in the technology and in people's scramble to embrace it—has been mind-boggling. But we're really just seeing the tip of the iceberg.

For one thing, we're not really "wired" yet. As Microsoft founder Bill Gates points out in his book, *The Road Ahead*, the true potential of the Web won't be realized until we have a global system of high-speed lines in place.

(Gates was uncharacteristically slow to see the impact the Web would have on the world. Since his moment of enlightenment, however, he's been moving at breakneck speed to try to gain domination in the browser market, going head-to-head against Netscape with his own Microsoft Explorer. His efforts have gained results. They've also gained the attention of federal antitrust investigators because of his practice of "bundling" the browser with Microsoft products. Other developments are also no doubt under way behind the company's doors. It will be interesting to see how much of a presence he can muster in cyberspace.)

At the moment, many domestic telephone companies, and certainly most services in foreign countries, rely on old-fashioned copper wires. While they're adequate for telephone service, they aren't real adept at handling the torrent of bytes of information that zip around the world every second of every day.

As a result, much of the system is operating at Model T speed. When the Web began to explode in popularity back in 1994 and 1995, one of the big jokes about it was the snail-like pace at which users would be connected to the sites they wanted to visit. As a result, it was frequently referred to as the World Wide Wait. At peak usage hours the information superhighway was much like the Los Angeles freeways at rush hour, a lot of people going nowhere fast. The bottlenecks were many, and it was often impossible to get connected at all.

It's getting better, but there is still wide disparity in the ease and speed with which people are able to get online. For a long time the luckiest users were probably those who worked for universities and major corporations and had access to the Web through their office computers. With direct high-speed ISDN connections, they could zip around the Web at will, gong from one site to another with the click of a button. Some universities had installed fiber-optic lines for their campus networks, speeding things up even further.

People who log on to the Web from home, on the other hand, have been limited by the speed of their modems, the devices that take the millions of bits of electronic information coming in through a user's phone line and translate them into text and graphics. As this book was being written, even the fastest modem could only transmit 56,000 bits per second, half the speed of an ISDN line.

But, again, this is all about to change. At the moment, the speed award goes to those lucky folks with cable television hookups. Cable modems are able to transmit 1.5 million bits per second. At that speed, moving through the Web is like flipping through the pages of a book.

Equally fast is a new system developed jointly by Microsoft, Compaq, Intel, and the nation's regional phone companies. Intended as a national standard for Web delivery, the asymmetrical digital subscriber line (ADSL) rivals cable modems for speed and works over standard telephone lines.

ADSL is cheaper and easier to install than cable—although it does require an expensive modem—and allows users to make phone calls while connected to the Web. It's also a continuous connection, eliminating the need to dial up a connection through a conventional modem or an Internet service provider. With the nationwide network of phone lines in place to handle ADSL service, I think it's only a matter of time before it becomes the nation's most common method of Web access.

WHAT'S NEXT?

The Web is becoming a remarkably profitable place to do business. But that doesn't mean every business needs to be there. Chapter 2 looks at the demographics of cyberspace and asks a few questions that will help you decide whether it's a place you and your business need to be.

2

·······································

IS THE WEB THE RIGHT PLACE FOR YOUR BUSINESS?

Before you continue your investigation into doing business in cyberspace, it's important to understand a few things. The Web is a brave new world where the rules are still a long way from being ironed out. It's a frontier littered with the digital skeletons of many business that have tried—and failed—to make money in cyberspace. Some went under because they didn't understand how to go about conducting business in this new environment; others because they didn't have the right product. Some failed for both reasons.

Like most new things, the Web has been accompanied by an enormous amount of hype. Lured by the excitement, many entrepreneurs quickly set up shop without doing the proper research. They didn't know if their products would sell in this new marketplace. They didn't know if their customers would be online and, if they were, if those customers would be able to find their businesses. They didn't understand advertising or marketing on the Web, and had no idea what their costs would be. Basically, they were flying blind, hanging out their digital signposts and hoping for the best.

Starting a business in cyberspace requires the same careful research you'd give any business. Success is not a sure thing, and although in many cases you can start a Web business for relatively little money, you can still lose everything you put into it. You need to take your time, consider the costs and the potential income, and plan accordingly.

As with any other business, you need to begin by analyzing

your product and your market. We'll begin with the biggest question of all.

IS THIS A VIABLE MEDIUM
FOR DOING BUSINESS?

We just learned that the Web has been accompanied by a lot of hype. Is it really the next big marketplace?

The answer is an unequivocal yes.

In 1995, when I was writing my book on mail order businesses, Web commerce was in its infancy (even now, it's little more than a toddler). Almost all the businesses online were quite small. Some were conventional storefront operations that had expanded into cyberspace. Others were run by former store owners like Jim Spitznagel, visionary people who saw the potential of this new medium and were willing to give it a shot.

At the time, the nation's premier mail order operators were reluctant to try doing business in cyberspace. This was certainly understandable. For them, creating the electronic equivalent of a sixty- or seventy-page color catalog is a major expense. One study of the industry at the time estimated it would cost more than $3 million a year to create and maintain a site large enough to offer the electronic equivalent of catalog shopping. So most of the biggies waited to see how things would shake out before they made the investment.

Then in early 1996 a very significant event occurred. Mail order giant L.L. Bean unveiled its Website (*http://www.llbean. com*). Close behind were Land's End (*http://www.landsend. com*), J. Crew (*http://www.jcrew.com*), Eddie Bauer (*http:// www.eddiebauer.com/*), and J. Peterman (*http://www.jpeterman. com/*).

For Web watchers, this was all the proof they needed that shopping on the Web was here to stay. It has certainly changed the face of the mail order industry. Many of us now rarely pick up a catalog, opting instead to sit at our computers, log on to the sites of our favorite businesses, and order merchandise with a few strokes of the keyboard.

As easy as 800 numbers are, ordering by computer is even

easier. You never get a busy signal or get put on hold until a customer service representative becomes available. Your order is delivered from your computer to the merchant's computer. There, it's printed out, processed, and your purchases are sent on their way to your doorstep. It's that simple.

HOW DIFFERENT IS IT?

In some ways, not at all. It's certainly an entirely new place to buy and sell, but the mechanics of the transactions aren't that different. Perhaps it's easiest to think of Web shopping as just another form of mail order. Customers still have to peruse a selection of items and send in an order, only now it's done electronically. So in that sense it's not real different from other forms of shopping.

What is different is that the democracy of the Web—the fact that anyone can have a presence there if they choose—has made going into business that much easier. Designing and printing a catalog, obtaining and constantly fine-tuning mailing lists, and sending the catalogs out makes conventional mail order an expensive business. People with little capital or no access to capital just can't get into the industry.

But the Web has leveled the playing field. Budding entrepreneurs with a good idea but not a whole lot of money can set up a Website fairly inexpensively. Once they're up and running, they're as easy to get to as L.L. Bean or any of the other giants.

There's still one big problem, of course. L.L. Bean already has millions of "real world" customers who can easily find the company's Web address in its catalogs or can look it up by conducting a Web search. (We'll talk more about these later. They're extremely important to small businesses on the Web.) The average ambitious young entrepreneur, on the other hand, is totally anonymous. Getting noticed is one of the big challenges in doing business on the Web. We'll take a look at advertising and marketing strategies that can help solve this problem later in the book.

WHY ARE PEOPLE ON THE WEB?

The growth of the Internet and the World Wide Web is one of the most significant cultural events in history. Estimates of the numbers of people on the Web vary, but the most reliable estimates put it at about fifty million.

But why are they there?

THEY WANT INFORMATION

This was the first reason for the popularity of cyberspace. Together, the Internet and World Wide Web are the most complete source of information that have ever existed. No matter what you're looking for, you'll be able to find both archival and up-to-the-minute data.

This is one reason wandering around the Web, or "surfing," is so much fun. You never know what you're going to stumble across. Following links from site to site can take you to places you never would have imagined, and the sense of expectation can keep users glued to their computers for hours on end.

The minutiae one can find is astonishing. I'm a fan of a data base called Papers that contains every article that's appeared in several dozen of the nation's leading newspapers dating back to the early '80s. Once you've selected the paper whose archives you want to explore, a simple keyword search will find all the articles with the keyword in them.

As an experiment, I went into the data base of the *Philadelphia Inquirer* and used my wife's maiden name to do a keyword search (her family lives in a Philadelphia suburb). Within seconds I was reading a little article about my father-in-law winning a golf tournament at his country club in 1987. Real estate transactions from the early '90s involving my two brothers-in-law were there, as were a number of brief "police blotter" articles that included the name of one of my wife's cousins, a police officer in a neighboring community.

In contrast to surfers, some people jump on the Web looking for specific information. Investors can follow market movements and make online trades. Scientists and academics can find endless information in their areas of expertise. Sports fans can get last night's scores and check out the current standings. People concerned about health and nutrition issues can get virtually any question answered by delving into data bases and Websites. If they can't find the answers there, there are several university-maintained sites that allow people to submit questions. The answers appear a few days later.

People also seek out information on products and services. One of my favorite stops on the Web is the Edmund's Automobile Buyers' Guide site (*http://www.edmunds.com/*). I was recently in the market for a used car for my daughter. A few visits to Edmund's gave me suggested wholesale and retail prices for all the candidates I was considering. The site also has extensive data on reliability and safety. It made the entire process extremely easy.

Cars are just one example of the thousands of products and services for which the Web can provide important consumer information. If you have the kind of product or service that generates calls from potential customers, having that information on a Website could be extremely important.

THEY WANT TO BE ENTERTAINED

This is the second reason the Web has become so popular. Surfing the Web is a lot of fun, and there's something for everybody. There are magazines, both electronic versions of the traditional paper variety and others, called "e-zines," that exist only in cyberspace. You can catch up on the news, the sports, and the weather. You can read book reviews and movie reviews and participate in online discussions about almost any topic under the sun. There are games and contests and free software you can download. There are stores and libraries and music. And there are the thousands, perhaps millions, of quirky home pages personally designed by individuals from all over the world.

THEY WANT TO BUY THINGS

This is the newest big activity on the Web, and the reason you bought this book. Although the Web is still used more as an advertising and marketing tool than it is for selling, the number of online vendors is increasing. And as we learned in the previous chapter, once the access inequities are addressed and people get used to the technology, it's going to explode.

WHAT'S BEING SOLD?

At this point it's safe to say that just about anything can be purchased on the Web. All the big retailers are online, of course, but there are also thousands of small businesses selling things that range from the rather pedestrian to the mind-boggling to the downright shocking. You can buy everything from Bibles to pornography (in 1998, 40 of the top 100 words used for Web searches were related to sex). For the Web surfer willing to do some serious exploring, there's a wealth of merchandise, not to mention entertainment, waiting to be discovered.

Trends in Web commerce have been charted since 1994, when researchers at the University of Michigan Business School surveyed 3,522 Web users in the United States and Europe. They found that the most frequent purchase was music, followed by home electronics, videos, travel services, tickets to entertainment events, and casual clothing. They also discovered that people more often used the Web to get information on products and services than they did to make purchases.

By the end of 1997, many of these same products were still popular, although their order had been switched somewhat. All told, more than $2.4 billion in goods and services were sold on the Web in 1997. Here are the leading categories of merchandise, by sales volume (in millions of dollars), for 1997, and the predicted totals for the year 2000.

	1997	2000
Computer hardware and software	$863	$2,901
Travel services	654	4,741
Entertainment	298	1,921
Books and music	156	761
Gifts, flowers, and greetings	149	591

Apparel and footwear	92	361
Food and beverages	90	354
Jewelry	38	107
Sporting goods	20	63
Consumer electronics	11	93
Other (home furnishings, toys, etc.)	65	197

And things got even better in 1998. Entering the year, some research firms predicted that sales would quadruple, pointing to the arrival of such big names as the Gap, Bloomingdale's, and Estée Lauder. They also felt that improved services such as online "shopping carts," passwords to preserve customer information, and easy-to-use links from other related sites and search engines would entice more people to shop online. By the end of the year, they predicted, as many as 26 million households would be shopping on the Web.

As it turns out, they were wrong. Sales didn't quadruple, but they did triple to nearly $8 billion. And there was nary a complaint to be heard. Web retailers were ecstatic with the results. A significant increase came during the holidays, when online sales of books, music, toys, and other popular gift items pushed online commerce to new heights. Between November 27 and December 24, 14.6 million people bought books, CDs, or videos on the Web (Amazon.com was the most popular site during the holidays, boasting a million first-time customers). More than 4 million bought toys and 3 million purchased apparel.

Obviously, there are some things that can't be purchased either through conventional mail order or on the Web. If you can't order it online, however, you can at least shop for it. For example, many realtors now have Web pages with photos and information on their current listings. Most have an e-mail connection, so if you're interested in learning more about a property you just fire off a quick message.

People are also shopping for cars in cyberspace, so much so that some experts are predicting the demise of hundreds of dealerships across the United States in the next five years. For car buyers, the availability of Websites where they can comparison shop has eliminated the need for driving from one dealer to another and the face-to-face dickering that so many people find annoying. Instead they can sit in front of their monitors and find the best deal.

One of the largest car-buying services on the Web is Auto-by-Tel *(http://autobytel.com/)*. The company represents approximately 2,700 dealers—an eighth of all the dealers in the nation. A buyer can log on to the site and go from dealer to dealer comparing prices. When he finds the car he wants, he finally makes the one real trip of the whole endeavor—to the dealer who has the vehicle he's selected. Because of the time and money they save, many buyers are willing to travel considerable distances, even several states away, to pick up their purchases.

WHAT ARE THE DEMOGRAPHICS OF THE WEB?

Any business concern has to pay attention to its market. Here are some of the significant demographic characteristics of Web users.

THEY'RE YOUNG

The average Web user is thirty-three years old. More than half of users are between twenty-five and forty-four.

THEY'RE EDUCATED AND AFFLUENT

Web users are well-educated and well-paid. Although the numbers differ a bit from one study to another, approximately half of Web users in 1997 had college degrees (compared to 28 percent of the population in general). About 60 percent of Web users worked in professional, technical, and managerial jobs. More than half had annual incomes above $50,000, and about a third made more than $70,000.

THERE ARE TWO MEN FOR EVERY WOMAN

But that's changing fast. The number of women on the Web has been steadily increasing since 1995, and it hasn't slowed down yet. A 1997 study by the Georgia Tech Research Corporation/ Graphic, Visualization, and Usability Center found that 38.4 percent of users were women, up from 31.7 percent in a study done a year earlier. A significant amount of the increase was among college-age women. Of the 10,000 participants in the survey, there were more female respondents in the sixteen- to twenty-year-old age range (11 percent) than males (8 percent).

AN INCREASING NUMBER ARE CHILDREN

In 1997, there were more than 9.8 million children using the Web in the United States, a 444 percent increase since 1995.

MANY PREFER THE WEB TO THE TUBE

More than a third of the respondents (35.2 percent) in the Georgia Tech study reported spending time on the Web instead of watching television on a daily basis. An additional 27 percent said they chose the Web over the TV at least once a week or more.

THEIR E-MAIL AND PHONE USE ARE EQUAL

Web users also reported using e-mail as often as they do the telephone.

THEY SPEND A LOT OF TIME ON THE WEB

About 40 percent of Web users spend from six to ten hours a week online and about 25 percent spend from eleven to twenty hours. More than 75 percent said they use their Web browsers daily. What are they doing there? Just fooling around, mostly. Almost 80 percent said they spend the majority of their time either browsing or looking for information.

DEMOCRATS HAVE THE EDGE OVER REPUBLICANS

The Georgia Tech study found that respondents were fairly polarized between the two major parties, with Democrats having the edge over Republicans, 40.7 to 34.1 percent. There was a slight increase in the percentage identifying themselves as Democrats since a study a year earlier. One interesting fact was that women were almost twice as likely to be associated with the Democratic party than the Republican party (50 percent vs. 27.6 percent). Among users fifty years and older, the proportion of Republicans and Democrats was almost identical (41.3 percent Republican vs. 41.1 percent Democrat).

When it came to voting, neither group were exactly model citizens. Of those respondents registered to vote, 59.6 percent had voted in the most recent local election, 57.9 percent in the most recent national election, and 50.7 percent in the most recent legislative election.

Age was found to play a direct role in voting behavior, with older users more likely to have voted in local, national, and legislative elections. Over a quarter of the nineteen- to twenty-five-year-old respondents reported not voting in any elections. Many younger users didn't note their party affiliation, despite reporting that they were registered to vote. No major gender differences were observed in any age groups.

They Prefer Letterman to Leno

One of the curious questions in the Georgia Tech study was on late night viewing habits. Of those respondents who included a late night talk show host preference, David Letterman was chosen more than twice as often as Jay Leno (55.4 percent for Letterman versus 24.8 percent for Leno). A higher percentage of women than men preferred Leno (28.2 percent female vs. 23.2 percent male). There were also marked distinctions based on age. Younger users tended to prefer Letterman, while older users preferred Leno.

They're Concerned About Privacy

Georgia Tech's 1997 study showed that privacy has replaced censorship as the number one policy concern of all Internet users. New users, in particular, were more cautious and concerned about their information being tracked for unknown purposes by Web server and Web page owners. Users across the board indicated they would like to see statements posted on Websites describing how information that's recorded will be used. This is not a difficult task for Website owners and Web service providers, and many have already taken steps to meet consumer concerns.

THEY'RE NOT ALL WEB SHOPPERS, AT LEAST NOT YET

The study also found disparities between seasoned Web users and novices in their attitudes toward shopping online. Eighty-four percent of veteran Web users reported having purchased goods over the Internet, as opposed to only 54 percent of new users. The most common reason given by new users for not shopping on the Web was the concern that their credit card numbers would not be secure. This was less of a problem for longtime Web users. Their main reason for not using the Internet to shop was the inability to judge the quality of products.

The reason most often given for using the Web for personal shopping was convenience (65 percent), followed by availability of product and vendor information (60 percent), the absence of pressure from sales people (55 percent), and saving time (53 percent). Males and females both ranked convenience first, but females slightly valued the absence of salespeople (54 percent) over product information (51 percent). Web veterans and respondents aged nineteen to fifty were more enthusiastic about Web shopping in all categories than were novice users and older respondents.

The most universal complaint about online shopping was slow speed. And again there were differences related to respondents' amount of experience with the Web. Among longtime users, 68 percent reported getting impatient and leaving a site before completing a transaction, as opposed to 38 percent of novices.

WHAT ARE THE DEMOGRAPHIC PROBLEMS?

The average Web user is young, educated, and affluent. This points to a few obvious problems.

THERE'S A GENERATION GAP

My mother owns a computer. It's sitting in a corner of her bedroom gathering dust. My in-laws own a computer. Theirs is sitting on a table in their basement covered with rolls of Christmas wrapping. The frightening thing is that by virtue of the fact that they even own computers, they're way ahead of most of their friends.

That my mother, my in-laws, and the vast majority of their friends are so disinterested in computers and technology points to one of the facts of life on the Web: the over sixty-five age group has largely been absent. This in itself is not a problem. Many folks feel there's enough traffic online already, thank you very much. As far as they're concerned, the geriatric set can stay out on the golf course.

But for people doing business on the Web, the absence of this demographic group is an enormous problem. My mother and my in-laws are prime examples of "Ikes," the generation of men and women who married, raised families, and enjoyed extremely prosperous careers in the years following the Second World War. They're the parents of the baby boom generation, and they'll probably go down in history as the wealthiest demographic group in the history of the nation.

Because of their economic successes, these people are voracious consumers. My in-laws, for example, just bought a new minivan. Why? The old one was two years old (or as my father-in-law jokes about all his trade-ins, "the ashtrays were full"). Time to trade it in. The fact that their old minivan was absolutely spotless, had less than 15,000 miles on it, and even still smelled brand new was immaterial. As far as they're concerned, every two years it's time for a new one.

As you can see, these folks like to spend money. And they're just the tip of the iceberg. Collectively, the over sixty-five set represents billions of dollars in annual buying power. But for the cybermerchant, they're largely out of reach. Finding ways to entice them into shopping on the Web is one of the biggest challenges facing Web businesses.

There are signs that more older people are beginning to come online. The 1997 Georgia Tech study found that the number of people over fifty on the Web increased from 11 percent in 1995 to 14 percent in 1997. As these numbers continue to rise, the online market for goods and services aimed at the senior set will also increase.

THERE'S AN INTIMIDATION FACTOR

This is probably the largest reason the over sixty-five group has been slow to embrace the Web. Let's face it, as people age, they become more set in their ways and see no reason to change. As I mentioned earlier, my mother has never learned to operate an ATM. She's afraid she'll "make a mistake" and somehow lose her money. My brother bought her a VCR for Christmas a few years ago. I'm not sure she's ever used it. She even has a CD player I helped her pick out, and the last time I visited her it wasn't even hooked up.

Is she a technophobe? Most definitely. But hers is a common reaction to technology among people of her age. They don't understand it, they're intimidated by it, and it's just easier to live without it.

But it's not just older people who can be slow to jump on the bandwagon. People of all ages can be a little intimidated. In fact, my initial reaction to computers and the Internet was a bit skittish. My first exposure was through my father, who was rare among his age group in that he was an early convert to the vast potential of cyberspace. A chemical engineer, he was used to technology and embraced new developments.

He bought his first computer, a Radio Shack TRS-80, in 1979. It was a plodding machine with 4 kilobytes of RAM. Floppy discs hadn't been invented yet, so he stored data on audiotape. Despite the machine's rather limited abilities, he was totally smitten and could spend hours in front of the thing.

Over the next decade, he continually upgraded his equipment to keep pace with the industry. He also managed to get an

Internet connection through a nearby university. He'd connect his telephone receiver to a modem, dial a few numbers, and, after a rapid series of beeps and boops from the modem filled the room, he'd be connected. The next thing I knew, we'd be looking at the vital statistics of some company he was thinking of investing in. We'd be able to see their profit and loss statements, chart their stock price, and even get vital information about the board of directors, including their home addresses. It seemed we could get everything but their hat sizes.

At that point I was mystified by the whole thing. I was still using a typewriter for writing, and everything about computers just baffled me. It wasn't until 1984 that I began using a computer at work, and we didn't get one for the house until 1992. Of course, by the time the Web was developed, I was a veteran, and eagerly jumped into cyberspace with both feet.

But the intimidation factor still exists and is a definite hindrance to doing business on the Web. Every person who's reluctant to learn how to use the technology is a lost customer. And there will be some who, for whatever reason, choose to stay away.

Just remember that the Web is still in its infancy in many ways, and there are more and more people coming online every day. When the Web started to take off in 1994, there were only a couple of million people connected. By 1998 there were as many as forty million. *That's a 2,000 percent increase in four years.* Those are the kind of numbers that will warm the heart of any merchant.

There's Also a Socioeconomic Gap

Another issue is the disparity between who has access to the Web and who doesn't. On the one hand, all you need to be a part of this wonderful new world is a computer, a modem, and a phone line. Just hook up a few wires, download some software, and you're ready to take off.

But how many people have computers these days? Fewer than you probably think. Since you've picked up this book, chances are you're in a socioeconomic class where home computers are as common as new cars. You or people you know may even have two or three around the house. And you probably spend at least part of your day in front of one at work.

But what we often forget is that we're still very much the exception rather than the rule. Even though they're cheaper than ever, computers are still an expensive item. For many families in the United States they're simply out of reach.

So, as in so many other aspects of American society, there's a serious gap between the haves and the have-nots, between those who have access to electronic information and those who don't.

If you pay attention to this issue, you'll recall Vice President Al Gore—an enthusiastic and knowledgeable advocate of the Web and electronic technology—and others referring to the haves as the "cognitive elite." And the have-nots? Well, let's just hope that ignorance is, indeed, bliss. For the cybermerchant, this disparity means there's another enormous group of potential customers who aren't able to shop in cyberspace.

What does all this demographic data mean to Web merchants? Well, despite his or her relatively young age, the average Web user is getting older. (When the Web first started becoming popular in 1994, the average user was of college age.) This means they're starting to buy houses and spend more money on big ticket items like appliances and furniture. Because they make good money, they also have more discretionary income for clothes, books, jewelry, travel, and other luxuries. And the steady increase in the number of women on the Web bodes well for online commerce.

Another good bit of news is the amount of time users spend online. As people spend time on the Web, they gradually begin to rely on the resources that are available to get information. You can get addresses and phone numbers, stay up-to-date on the standings in professional sports, track the movement of the stock market, and obtain information on an almost infinite number of other topics. Learning to shop there is just a logical extension of that behavior, so most novice Web users will become comfortable with the idea of online shopping eventually.

Also encouraging is the reported use of e-mail. The fact that e-mail use is on a par with phone use paints a tremendously strong picture of the rapid integration of the Internet and the Web into the daily lives of those who currently use it.

The concerns expressed in the Georgia Tech study, on the other hand, show that there are still serious hurdles to overcome. Worries over stolen credit card numbers are still a universal complaint. In fact, as we'll see, this is such a nonissue that it's almost laughable.

A more legitimate concern is the "tracking" of user behavior and habits, which, understandably, people see as an invasion of their privacy. Some of this is related to the use of what are known as "cookies." We'll look at these later in the book as well.

The limited age range is another concern. The Web is still largely the domain of young people, so companies that target older customers are at a disadvantage. While it's a great medium for selling electronics, sporting goods, compact discs, and clothing, it will be a while before hearing aids and orthopedic shoes are big sellers.

HOW WILL THE DEMOGRAPHICS CHANGE?

I once interviewed Peter Francese, the founder and former publisher of *American Demographics* magazine, for an article I was writing on the impact of an aging baby boom generation on the health care industry. Will there be a strain on services, I asked him, and will we be able to afford them?

"Never underestimate the ability of entrepreneurs to find their way to your doorstep," he replied. "We will have the services we need at prices we can afford."

This is the same reason that inequity in access to information technology will soon no longer be an issue. You'll recall that I mentioned the abhorrent attitude many Internet jockeys had toward the idea that the Web would ever be used for commerce. Well, they're long gone. There's an electronic stampede going on right now that makes the California gold rush look like a stroll in the park. There's so much money to be made on the Web that entrepreneurs are falling all over each other trying to find their way to our electronic doorsteps. So far they've been limited by the size of the market, which in turn has been limited by the access issues we just discussed. But that's all going to change, and soon.

The reason? Cable television companies and telephone companies.

Think about it. Although computers are still the exception rather than the rule in American homes, almost everyone has a television. And an awful lot of those televisions are hooked up to cable systems that deliver their programming. Without even knowing it, the companies that have been wiring the nation for cable television over the last fifteen or twenty years have been creating a system for Internet and Web access. Once they start offering Web access, it won't matter whether a home has a computer or not. The signal will be delivered straight to their TVs.

Phone companies are even better prepared to provide Internet access. Most of the information that flows across the Web already travels on conventional telephone wires. It hasn't taken the phone companies long to realize that providing Internet access could be an extremely profitable venture, and they're rapidly moving in that direction.

For consumers, the arrival of cable companies and telephone companies into the fray can only be good news. Competition will drive down prices (in theory anyway) and anyone will be able to get online for just a few dollars a month. Regardless of who provides your service, you'll have the choice between having your Internet signal delivered to your computer, to your television, or to both. Families that don't have a computer will be given a control box for their television that will allow them to roam about cyberspace.

Families in a few cable markets have had cable connections to the Web since 1997. For many others the new technology is just around the corner. In January 1998 seven cable companies spent $350 million for 850,000 specially designed digital cable boxes with built-in computer processors and cable modems. Their plan was to distribute the boxes to as many as 500,000 customers in twenty-seven cities around the country by the end of the year. Users would enjoy all the benefits of the Web, including e-mail.

The manufacturer of the units, veteran cable box manufacturer Scientific Atlanta, claimed at the time to have an eighteen-month lead on the rest of the industry. That drew an immediate retort from their main rival, General Instrument, which announced plans to have their own product on the market within a few months.

WILL THEY USE IT?

The Web so far has largely been a place for young, educated, and affluent consumers who, through their jobs or their socio-economic clout, have been privy to this wonderful new technology. In the meantime, the less fortunate have been left spinning their wheels. But that's going to quickly change as cable companies and telephone companies make Web access easier.

It won't be long before the majority of Americans will be able to sit in front of their televisions or computers and, either through a cable modem or an ADSL line, do all sorts of electronic tasks. They'll be able to shop, order groceries and have them delivered to their homes, pay their bills, do their banking, buy and sell securities, and even talk to each other and see each other on their screens while they chat.

So, yes, the demographic base of the Web will grow. There's no question about it. The American who doesn't have access to the Web will soon be the exception rather than the rule.

But that's just half the battle. Remember the old saying, "You can lead a horse to water but you can't make him drink?" Well, the horses will be at the watering hole, but whether or not they'll drink is another matter altogether. Getting people accustomed to new ways of doing things is difficult. Some people are intimidated by technology, and getting them to use the Web is going to be a challenge. (Just remember my mother and her fear of using ATMs.) That's why changing consumer behavior, not access to the technology, is the biggest challenge facing Web entrepreneurs. The Web won't achieve its true potential until it's used equally by people from all socioeconomic groups and all age groups.

ARE YOUR CUSTOMERS ON THE WEB?

If they're not, you're wasting your time. But if they are, you need to be there, too. Here are some of the markets that are easily accessible on the Web.

COLLEGES AND UNIVERSITIES

America's campuses are wired, as are those in Canada, Europe, and Australia. Colleges and universities in Asia, Africa, and South America have been slower to get online but they're catching up. Almost every person associated with a college or university has an e-mail address, so this is an enormous market for a wide variety of goods and services.

BUSINESSES

American businesses have been scrambling all over one another, and spending millions of dollars in the process, to establish Websites. It's virtually impossible to find a Fortune 500 company these days that isn't online. Many smaller companies have been equally quick to set up sites.

If you have a product or service that's purchased by these businesses, not being online could spell disaster. The following industries have been among the leaders in venturing into cyberspace.

- Technology
- Entertainment
- Publishing
- Travel-related businesses
- Book and music retailing
- Accounting
- Investments
- Utility companies
- Petroleum-related businesses

It's also important to look at whether individual companies will continue to operate their Websites. The leap into cyberspace by American businesses has raised the question of whether these companies are finding their investments worthwhile. Although some are selling merchandise online, for most it has been an extremely expensive form of advertising and public relations. They're on the Web because it's there and because everyone else is doing it. Researchers are beginning to examine the impact of Websites on companies and organizations, and they feel there may be a shaking out as some decide they're not worth the time and expense.

Government Agencies

To its credit, the United States government has been surprisingly nimble in adopting Web technology. Just about all federal offices and departments have Websites. Even the White House can be accessed via the Web. Businesses buy and sell from one another online. Government agencies can be customers, too.

WHAT ARE BUSINESSES USING THE WEB FOR?

The most obvious use is selling merchandise. You need to make a buck, right? But outright selling is still the exception rather than the rule. Here are some of the other tasks businesses are accomplishing with their Websites:

- Market research
- Public relations
- Advertising
- Customer service
- Product information
- Product promotion
- Media relations

- Technical service
- Intracompany communications (intranets)

ARE YOUR COMPETITORS ON THE WEB?

If they are, you'd better get hopping. When L.L. Bean unveiled its Website in early 1996, I checked to see what their competitors were doing. Only Land's End had a comparable site. J. Crew was working on one but at that point they just had a single page listing the company's name, address, and a toll-free number. All the others were nowhere to be found. Within a few months they all had sites.

Roam around the Web to see if businesses like yours are already there. Monitor their sites for a while and see how they develop. If you see them growing and becoming more complex, that's a good sign they're finding the Web a good place to do business, and a good reason for you to jump on board.

WHAT WILL IT COST TO PUT YOUR BUSINESS ON THE WEB?

The Web is the great equalizer. With a little effort and creativity, you can create a Website for next to nothing. If you have access to the right software, you can even do it yourself. The hypertext markup language coding required to create a site is not difficult to learn, and if you have access to a scanner, you can add graphics and photographs of your merchandise. That's enough to give you a bare-bones site. Beyond that, you can become as fancy as you care to.

If you have the money in your start-up budget, you can hire someone to create your site. Website design is an enormous business these days, and prices are all over the place. I've seen figures ranging from $800 a page to hourly fees as low as $20. I've heard of people getting a site set up for $300. I've also read that a large corporation or catalog business like L.L. Bean can spend up to $3 million to build their sites. We'll look at getting your site designed in detail in Chapter 6.

CAN THE WEB HELP YOU CUT COSTS?

In November 1997, the San Francisco *Chronicle* ran an article about a company called Cisco Systems Inc. According to the article, the high-tech firm, which manufactures computer networking equipment and is 50 percent larger than its six leading rivals combined, was doing more than $7 million worth of business a day just on their Website. The article also said the company saves $270 million a year in salaries, software distribution, and paperwork costs by operating on the Web.

Can the Web be a shortcut to savings for your business? Chances are it can. At the very least, e-mail can reduce your long-distance phone charges, fax costs, and the amount you spend sending information via the U.S. Postal Service. For example, rather than mailing customers frequently requested printed material, you could simply put it on your Website and let them download it. Bills and business letters could be sent via e-mail rather than through the post office. The savings can quickly add up.

A QUICK LOOK AT THREE ONLINE BUSINESSES

There are tens of thousands of businesses operating on the Web. They range from electronic Mom and Pop ventures operating out of basements, attics, and spare bedrooms to capital intensive behemoths that probably will be in business for five years or more before they turn a profit. Here are three examples—one huge site, one medium-sized, and one very small.

AMAZON.COM (*http://www.amazon.com*)

We'll start with one of the biggest sites on the Web. With more than 2.5 million titles, Amazon.com is the Web's first discount book "superstore." It's also the first megabusiness started exclusively for the Web. It was so expensive to create, its founders had to enlist the financial backing of some of the same venture capitalists that bankrolled many of the most well-known high-tech start-ups in Silicon Valley.

This enormous site has numerous features that set the standard for online shopping ease. It allows users to search for books by title, author, or subject. When you select a book, you can read reviews that have appeared in the media and get all the pertinent information about the book—publisher, publishing date, ISBN, current availability, and both the publisher's retail price and Amazon's discounted price. Sometimes there are interviews with a book's author. It also has a "shopping basket" option that allows shoppers to amass a list of selections as they move through the site. You can review and delete items from your shopping basket before you "check out."

I find Amazon.com, and similar sites that have followed it on to the Web, amazing for the sheer amount of inventory it carries and the incredible amount of cross-linking that its designers have thought up. Each of the 2.5 million books can be called up by entering the title or author's name into a search file. There are bestseller lists in dozens of categories. Visitors can enter their own reviews of books they've read, which are then available for other Amazon.com visitors to read, and authors can also enter remarks about the books they've written.

Once you've made a purchase from the company, all your ordering information—name, address, and credit card number—is kept on file to facilitate subsequent purchases. When you return to the site, a link with your name on it will take you to a list of suggestions prepared by the company's computers and based on the subject matter of your previous purchases. It's a fascinating site and one I enjoy just roaming around in, even when I'm not in the market for anything.

Amazon.com is probably the largest company to be formed specifically for the Web. It has no storefront counterpart nor does it distribute a printed catalog. Most other sites of comparable size have been created by companies that already had large catalog businesses, such as L.L. Bean and Eddie Bauer. Industry watchers are waiting to see what will happen now that large "real world" book companies like Barnes & Noble have come online with their own sites. Some speculate that their sheer size and financial resources will make it hard for Amazon.com to compete. It will be an interesting battle to watch.

Although it has enjoyed steadily rising revenues, Amazon.com has yet to make a profit (it's projected to lose $80 million in 1999). Its hardware and software costs are extremely high, and it has an army of technicians to keep everything running correctly. The company's future success will certainly serve as a barometer for big businesses that have made the move into cyberspace.

ESKIMO JOE'S (*http://www.eskimojoes.com/*)

Every college town has its popular hangout. Since 1975 the place to be for the 18,000 students at Oklahoma State University in Stillwater, Oklahoma, has been Eskimo Joe's. The sprawling two-story restaurant/bar has several dining rooms, three or four bars, and a big menu featuring many creative variations on the standard fare of burgers, chicken, salads, and fries. The place is always busy, especially on weekends. Its success has inspired its owners to open two other restaurants in town, a popular Mexican eatery called Mexico Joe's and an upscale dining room called Stillwater Bay.

But perhaps the most interesting thing about Eskimo Joe's is the thriving international business it has cultivated in Eskimo Joe's apparel. You can travel in Europe, Japan, and even Australia and have a pretty good chance of running into someone wearing an Eskimo Joe's T-shirt, hat, or other garment. The restaurant sells some merchandise out of a shop attached to the restaurant and has another retail outlet in an Oklahoma City mall. It also has a thriving international mail order business. I would be surprised if its sales from apparel don't exceed those from the restaurant.

Eskimo Joe's launched its extensive Website in October 1997. It offers all the same merchandise that's carried in its catalog. Customers can use a sophisticated ordering system that includes a shopping cart feature and secure, encrypted ordering via Netscape and Microsoft Explorer browsers. America Online customers can order using an unsecured server. The site has been certified as a "safe shopping site" by Public Eye, an Internet organization that tests, certifies, and monitors the reliability of online businesses.

The Eskimo Joe's site is an excellent example of a mid-sized business that has made a seamless entry into cyberspace. The site is well thought out and easy to navigate, and the site designers have done an excellent job anticipating customer questions, particularly those regarding ordering procedures and security issues. Although the start-up costs clearly were many times those of smaller businesses like Hillendale, the golf course site I discuss next, the company's international reputation and ability to advertise its Website through its print catalogs will certainly help it recoup its investment.

HILLENDALE GOLF COURSE (*http://www.hillendale.com*)

"I just sent off two golf bags to New Zealand, and I don't have the slightest idea how the customer found us," marvels Mary Novickas, the owner of Hillendale Golf Course, a scenic, rolling eighteen-hole layout near Ithaca in New York's Finger Lakes region. "Here we are in this small town in upstate New York, and we're getting orders over the Web from people halfway around the world. It's amazing."

Novickas, an LPGA professional who once came close to earning a spot on tour, has owned Hillendale since 1983. When she bought it, it was a nine-hole track with a reputation for being something of a cow pasture. The fairways, wet and muddy from snow melt at the beginning of each season, were hard as a rock and pretty much burned out by midsummer. The greens and clubhouse were equally shabby.

Since she's owned it, Novickas has turned Hillendale into one of the most popular golf courses in the area. The original front nine now boasts healthy, carefully groomed fairways, and she's added a challenging back nine on adjacent property she bought in the late '80s. She's installed a watering system, a large putting green with a practice sand trap, and beautifully carved granite yardage markers at each tee box. The course has been named one of the top ten women-friendly courses in North America by *Golf for Women* magazine.

Novickas also does a big business in her pro shop, which has been upgraded along with the rest of the course. She carries many of the best names in equipment—including Callaway, Cobra, Taylor, Titleist, Ping, Cleveland, and Square Two—and offers a wide selection of woods, irons, putters, balls, bags, shoes, apparel, and other merchandise. Her prices are among the best in the area and her shop has become increasingly popular each year.

Novickas launched her Website in 1996. The site is nicely designed and easy to navigate. It offers general information about the course, a calendar of events, and a tour of the course with diagrams and photographs of each hole. It also has a link to the pro shop, and online orders now account for more than 30 percent of her business.

The pro shop's phone number is listed so customers can place orders over the phone. There's also a toll-free "Golf Supply Hotline." But for customers who want to order over the Web, the process is a bit fuzzy (we'll look at online ordering systems later in the book). There is an e-mail link that can be used, but it offers no instructions or formatted boxes in which to include information about the items to be ordered or the method of payment. Customers typically send a message describing the merchandise they want to buy, and the pro shop staff responds with questions about method of payment and shipping instructions. Novickas says that operating this way has not been a problem. In fact, she feels it allows her and her staff to provide better service.

"We like to communicate with customers about their purchases to make sure they're getting the kind of equipment they need," she says. "Rather than just take an order and send it out, we can discuss their purchases with them beforehand. We get 90 percent of our orders from the Website via e-mail, and no one has complained about the system."

Like Jim's Ithaca Music Shop, the Hillendale Website is a good example of how a small business can create a site with a minimal investment (about $2,000) and low overhead ($50 a month). Novickas is exploring ideas for expansion of the site and hopes to streamline her online ordering process. She's also looking into the viability of offering online video instruction.

WHAT'S NEXT?

If they're not already, it's time to get your feet wet and take the plunge into cyberspace. The Web is a fascinating place, with its own language and customs. Moving around also requires special navigational tools. We'll take a quick tour of the Web in Chapter 3.

FOR MORE INFORMATION

Here are a few Websites that will give you more information on what kinds of businesses are on the Web, as well as some additional demographic information.

➡ **Catalog Site** (*http://www.catalogsite.com*) This site maintains an extensive list of more than 100 companies doing business both in conventional mail order and on the Web. It also provides links to their Websites.

➡ **WebAccess** (*http://webcommerce.com/webaccess/webcomrc.html*) This site is maintained by Web Access and describes the commercial and marketing opportunities available on the Web. It also has a set of links for those who want to do further investigation.

➡ **Graphic, Visualization, and Usability Center WWW User Survey** (*http://www.cc.gatech.edu/gvu/user_surveys*) Visiting the Georgia Tech Research Corp./Graphic, Visualization, and Usability Center site will provide you with the chance to examine the results of their surveys in detail.

➡ **CommerceNet/Nielsen Internet Demographics Survey** (*http://www.nielsenmedia.com/interactive/commercenet/*) The A.C. Nielsen Company (yes, the same one that studies television) has also analyzed the demographics of Web users.

➡ **Cyberatlas: The Reference Desk for Web Marketing** (*http://www.cyberatlas.com*) Cyberatlas is another good source of both demographic data and general trends in cyber commerce.

3

LEARNING YOUR WAY AROUND CYBERSPACE

Depending on the degree of experience you have with the Web, you may or may not need to read this chapter. It briefly describes the basics of moving about cyberspace and how to find the many resources available on the Web. The tools I describe are those available on Netscape, which is one of the most commonly used browsers on the Web and the one with which I'm most familiar.

WHAT IS A WEBSITE?

A Website is a collection of information on the World Wide Web that can be accessed by typing in a series of keyboard commands. These keystrokes are called a "universal resource locator," or "URL," and are, in effect, the address of the Website. In fact, the term "Web address" has become synonymous with URL.

The information in a Website appears in a page format on users' monitors. Each page has its own URL, which makes it distinct from every other point in cyberspace. There can be one page of information on a site or there can be tens of thousands or more. The information is presented as text and graphics, and users can move from page to page much as they would if they were reading a book

As an online business owner, you'll operate a Website whose

pages contain your merchandise, order forms, and other information related to your business.

YOU BEGIN AT "HOME"

Web browsers like Netscape allow users to customize the way Web pages will appear on their computer monitors. For example, you can specify a certain typeface and type size. You can choose to have just text appear (which will speed things up quite a bit, by the way). You can even select the color of your text.

You can also pick a site that will automatically appear when you open your browser. That site is known as "Home," and you can return to it from anywhere on the Web by clicking on the "Home" button on the browser's tool bar. If you wish, you can also just have a blank page appear when you open your browser.

USING LINKS

Links are electronic shortcuts that make getting from one Web address to another as simple as pointing and clicking your mouse. A link appears on a Web page as either text or a graphic with a line beneath it. The text can be the name of a site or it can be the site's actual URL. By clicking on the text or graphic, your browser immediately takes you to that site. Most links appear in blue text until they're clicked, at which point they turn red or violet.

Links can take users from page to page within a Website. They also can take users from one site to another. They're easy to create. It's just a matter of making a few keyboard commands. Almost all people who maintain their own Web sites have created links to other sites they find interesting. As we'll see later in the chapter, links are also used by online directories to help Web users find information on specific topics.

As an online business owner, you'll find that links can be a good way to bring more customers to your site. We'll discuss how they can be used later in the book.

WHAT'S NEW? WHAT'S COOL?

Almost all Web directory sites, including Netscape, have *What's New?* and *What's Cool?* sections to show off new additions and share other sites they think will be of interest to their visitors. For the novice Web user these can be a useful first step in discovering what's out there.

DOING A SEARCH

The Web is like the largest library you can imagine. There's information on everything, available from a seemingly infinite number of resources. The challenge is finding what you're looking for.

This is where search tools come into play. The Netscape browser's tool bar has a "Net Search" option that will connect you to sites like Lycos, Excite, Yahoo, and Infoseek. These are electronic directories that allow you to find information in several ways. One option is to click on one of the many categories—such as health, computers, sports, and personal finance—that will appear on the screen. A new page opens with links to various sources of information within that topic.

For example, clicking on the "Health" link in Infoseek takes you to a page with twenty-two links to health-related topics such as dentistry, insurance, mental health, family health, and smoking. Clicking on those links takes you further into each subject area. Eventually you'll end up with direct links to sites that can provide you with information on a specific topic.

Another way to get information is to do a "key word' search. You type a key word or words into a small dialogue box on the screen, hit a "search" or "seek" button, and in just seconds you'll have a list of Web pages that contain the key words.

All search directories operate a bit differently from one another. You'll want to experiment a bit with each one to find out which one you prefer.

BOOKMARKS

For me, bookmarks are one of the really great features about browsers. A bookmark is a site whose Web address is stored by your computer. You can then open the site by scrolling to it using the "Bookmarks" option that appears in the control panel at the top of your computer screen. It saves having to type in the address of a site every time you open it.

To create a bookmark, all you have to do is open the site whose address you want to have stored and select "Add Bookmark" under the bookmark option. If you're like most people, you'll begin to have so many bookmarks it can become a bit unwieldy. To organize your bookmarks, you can divide them into separate sections by using a control panel that opens when you select "View Bookmarks." The control panel also allows you to delete bookmarks from your list.

Most people bookmark sites for both work and personal use. For example, among the dozens of sites I have bookmarked are Oklahoma State University, where my daughter attends college; Amazon.com, the online bookstore we discussed in Chapter 2; a variety of federal agency sites that I sometimes use to gather data for writing projects; Thomas, a link to the legislative branch of the federal government; College and University Home Pages, a site that has links to more than 3,000 colleges and universities around the world; Excite, which is one of the best search sites on the Web; WeatherNet, a site that provides up-to-the minute weather conditions and forecasts for the entire United States; and Golf Web, a site with tons of information on current tournaments and other golf-related topics.

E-MAIL

This is the original and most widely used Internet tool. E-mail (electronic mail) allows you to send messages and correspondence to anyone in the world practically at the speed of light. For many people, e-mail has become the preferred method of communicating, both in their professional and their personal lives.

Everyone with e-mail has an electronic address that others use to send them messages. People who have e-mail through their jobs have a three-letter suffix at the end of their addresses that describes the nature of their employer's activities. For example, the addresses of people who work in higher education end in "edu"—*johnbrown@yale.edu.* Those who work for for-profit businesses have addresses ending in "com"—*johnbrown @ibm.com.* The addresses of people who work for nonprofits end in "org"—*johnbrown@redcross.org.*

Many people who have their e-mail service through a commercial provider like America Online or any of the hundreds of local providers that dot the country have addresses that end with the service provider's name and "com"—*johnbrown@aol. com*—or "net"—*johnbrown@stargazer.net.*

The @ sign in these addresses is the equivalent of the word "at" and the period is pronounced "dot." So if John Brown the Yale professor were giving someone his e-mail address, he'd tell them, "It's John Brown at Yale dot edu."

Using E-mail

People use e-mail for all the same things for which they use the phone or "snail mail" (regular mail delivered by the post office). They have business-related exchanges, they send important documents, they gossip, they exchange recipes, they send birthday greetings, they argue, and they make appointments and lunch dates and dinner dates.

They also pass on information from one person to another, including jokes. In fact, the use of e-mail and the Internet to pass on humor has been one of the most fascinating aspects of the technology. These days, when a high-profile incident occurs, such as the furor over the relationship between President Clinton and White House intern Monica Lewinsky, jokes about it spread across the country like wildfire. I've e-mailed jokes to friends immediately after getting them, only to discover they'd already received them from other friends. In some cases the jokes came from the same people who sent them to me in the first place.

For people who do business on the Web, e-mail can be quite useful. For one thing, it's easier than regular mail. Rather than writing a letter, printing it out, stuffing it in an envelope, sticking on a stamp, and walking to the mailbox, you just hit a button and your missive arrives on the desktop of its recipient in seconds.

E-mail also has advantages over the telephone. You never get a busy signal and it doesn't matter if the recipient is out of the office when you send a message. It will be there waiting when they return. People also tend to use e-mail to send little messages they'd never bother to communicate over the phone.

E-mail also helps create closer relationships. There's something about the back-and-forth nature of the medium that builds a rapport between people. Part of it is the immediacy e-mail offers. You can have a conversation about a topic that is close to a face-to-face conversation—brief one- or two-sentence exchanges that have a certain intimate quality. The fact that romances and even marriages have been fostered by e-mail certainly proves this point.

USENET

Long before the Web became a great resource for shopping and looking up information it was an electronic gathering place for people interested in discussing topics in which they shared an interest. Although it doesn't get as much attention as the glitzier aspects of the Web, this type of activity is still as popular as ever.

Collectively these discussion groups, or "newsgroups" (there are more than 40,000 of them), comprise the Usenet. Members of a newsgroup read each other's postings and then add their own opinions. Some newsgroups are open, meaning all messages get posted. Others are refereed, moderated by individuals who weed out postings that are inappropriate or off-the-topic.

Because of the anonymity involved, most members of a newsgroup tend to say what they really think, and some of the online behavior and language gets a bit heated. These angry messages are called "flames" (see the section on Netiquette at the end of this chapter) and can be as nasty and off-color as any verbal assault you've ever heard.

Your access to the Usenet will depend on how you're hooked up to the Internet. If you go through a commercial service provider, for example, the company will select which newsgroups to make available to its customers. Most will weed out any whose subject matter is deemed offensive or inappropriate. If you have a direct connection through a university or some other entity, however, you'll have much wider access.

Although I've never posted a message to a newsgroup, I have spent a fair amount of time reading other people's postings (this makes me a "lurker," the Usenet version of a peeping Tom). During the O. J. Simpson trial, I regularly logged on to a newsgroup that featured lively debate over Simpson's innocence or guilt. Although there was the usual amount of loony ranting and raving, there were also surprisingly thoughtful discussions of race, the evidence, the double standards that exist in meting out justice to the wealthy and connected, and the many other issues that surrounded the trial. It was generally fascinating reading.

To some degree the Usenet can be a marketing tool for people selling goods and services on the Web. However, this must be accompanied by great delicacy. Many people in newsgroups react with enormous hostility to any commercial activity, and you can find yourself on the receiving end of thousands of flames if you're not careful. We'll look at using the Usenet in your business later.

MAILING LISTS

Mailing lists are wonderful tools for receiving information that can be important to your business. They're quite similar to Usenet groups. The difference is that you have to enter a Usenet group to download messages, while people "subscribe" to a mailing list and have messages automatically delivered to an electronic "mailbox" on their computer. All mailing lists have administrators whose job is to make sure everything runs smoothly and deal with any technical problems members are having.

Mailing lists are often used by small numbers of people and usually focus on a single topic. For example, I have at various times subscribed to mailing lists on both fiction writing and screen writing. I found them interesting for a time but I also was overwhelmed by the number of messages that would appear. It wasn't unusual for me to arrive at work and find forty or fifty messages that had been posted to the list overnight. It became physically impossible to read them all and I eventually unsubscribed from the lists.

Some mailing lists are public, meaning anyone can join, and others are private, demanding certain requirements of their members. They can also be either moderated or unmoderated. Messages submitted to moderated lists are evaluated by a sort of gatekeeper who reads the messages and then only posts those deemed pertinent and acceptable. He or she may also edit messages and create a digest of messages on the list. In an unmoderated site, as you've no doubt guessed, anything goes. All messages are posted no matter how absurd or off-the-topic they may be.

One thing I found interesting with mailing lists was that, much as in real life, conversation often tended to be dominated by three or four know-it-alls who, also as in real life, I quickly found immensely annoying. They would post far more messages than anyone else and would also get into arguments with one another that could quickly degenerate into flame wars. I can't say I always learned a whole lot from my mailing list buddies, but for sheer entertainment value, logging on was frequently worth the effort.

For businesses, mailing lists can have many benefits in terms of keeping in touch with customers. They can serve as electronic bulletin boards to post product and technical information. They can be used to seek feedback on products and services. Some businesses use them to send out electronic newsletters.

Some also use them to compare notes on shared business-related issues such as advertising and marketing.

SUBSCRIBING TO A MAILING LIST

It's easy. Usually it's as simple as sending a message to the list's mail server with the word "subscribe" and the list's E-mail address in the body of the message. To have your name removed from a list, you might follow the same procedure using the word "unsubscribe." Of course, some lists have more complex commands. Generally, upon subscribing to a list you'll receive an automated message detailing the commands for the list.

There are three important addresses every mailing list member must have. One is the address of the automated list server, which you need to subscribe and unsubscribe; the second is the address to which you send messages that will appear in the mailboxes of all the other members of the list; and the third is the address of the list administrator, who you'll need to contact if you have problems sending or receiving information.

FOLLOWING THE PROPER "NETIQUETTE"

One of the fascinating things about electronic communication is the way certain rules of behavior, or "netiquette," have evolved. Because communication on the Internet is accomplished almost exclusively with the written word (for the moment, anyway), it lacks the tones of voice, facial expressions, and body language that accompany face-to-face discussions. As a result, subtle nuances of meaning are difficult to achieve and it's easy for people to misunderstand each other. What's meant as humor, for instance, can easily be interpreted as meanness or criticism. It's not surprising, then, that these rules have evolved. Here are a few of the basics.

ALL CAPS ARE A NO-NO

Don't send messages in all capital letters BECAUSE IT'S CONSIDERED SHOUTING! It's okay to use them from time to time to emphasize a point, but sending an entire message in caps is definitely a serious breach of netiquette.

USE EMOTICONS TO INDICATE EMOTION

You can use what are called "emoticons" to get the tone of your message across. These are little facial expressions you can make with keyboard characters. For example, to indicate happiness, satisfaction, or that a statement is meant as a joke, you can make this character :-) using a colon, dash, and close parentheses. If you tilt your head to the left, you'll see a smiling face. Unhappiness is denoted with :-(. A wink is another common emoticon and is expressed like this ;-).

These three are probably the most commonly used emoticons, but there are many more, some of which are extremely clever. To see a thorough list, visit *http://wwws.enterprise.net/fortknox/ emoticon/smiley.html*.

NO SPAMMING

Spamming is a practice where an entire network is flooded with the same message. It's a common form of advertising— the equivalent of junk mail, really—and is every bit as annoying as those sales calls you get at home in the evening when you're just sitting down to dinner. The practice has already drawn the attention of the Federal Trade Commission, which has held hearings on the subject to investigate the possible need for regulation of mass mailings on the Web.

NO FLAMING

A flame is an angry, derogatory, or malicious message directed at another person. They are commonly found in Usenet groups where people will have online discussions on a whole variety of topics. The anonymity and physical distance afforded by these environments cause people to say things they'd probably never say in a face-to-face encounter (many of them would probably end up with a black eye if they did), and some of the back and forths can get quite hostile.

FOR MORE INFORMATION

Here are some good books and two Websites that can help you learn more about life on the Web:

➡ *The Usenet Book* by Bryan Pfaffenberger (Addison-Wesley, 1995)
➡ *Netiquette* by Virginia Shea (Albion Books, 1994)
➡ *Your Internet Consultant: The FAQs of Life Online* by Kevin Savetz (Sams Publishing, 1994)
➡ *Free $tuff from the Internet* by Patrick Vincent (Coriolis Group Books, 1994)
➡ **Global Network Navigator** *http://gnn.com/gnn/GNNhome. html*
➡ **Electronic Fronteir Foundation** *http://www.eff.org/*

WHAT'S NEXT?

As I pointed out earlier, the Web may be a decidedly different place to conduct business, but that doesn't mean that conventional business strategies don't apply. As with any commercial venture, the first step in creating a business in cyberspace is to create a business plan. That's the topic of Chapter 4.

4

CREATING YOUR DIGITAL BUSINESS PLAN

The Web is a different business environment. That, we all understand. But that doesn't mean standard business procedures don't apply. You would never think of starting a conventional storefront or mail order business without careful planning. Starting a business online requires the same amount of attention.

Yet, as amazing as it seems, many companies, from major corporations to basement entrepreneurs, have failed to follow this most basic of rules. Failure to create a thorough plan is the biggest reason online businesses go under. The Web has generated a lemminglike behavior that has companies stumbling all over one another in their efforts to establish a presence in cyberspace. But in their excitement, they've put the cart before the horse. "We need a Website," they tell themselves, and the next thing you know, they have one. Then they stand around scratching their heads and wondering what to do next.

The success of your online venture lies in careful analysis and preparation. This chapter will take you through the necessary steps for planning your Web business. We'll begin by asking a very important question.

WHY DO YOU WANT TO BE ON THE WEB?

As I just mentioned, for many companies that have failed at online commerce, the answer to this question was, "Because it's there!"

Wrong answer.

If you're running a business, being on the Web should either help you increase sales, reduce expenses, or both. It's that simple.

This doesn't necessarily mean you need to be selling goods and services from your Website. Some companies use their sites as very effective marketing and advertising tools by just including information about themselves and their products and services. In fact, there are more businesses using the Web for these functions than there are for selling. Using this new medium gives them better exposure to their customers. If people want to make purchases from these companies, they can contact them using information that's also contained on the site.

Here are some other important considerations for business people who think they might want to be online.

WILL IT INCREASE SALES?

Always the best reason for undertaking any new business strategy. Being on the Web certainly gives you a larger customer base than operating out of a storefront. Jim Spitznagel thinks about that every time he sends off a bunch of compact discs to Japan or Argentina. If being on the Web means you can increase your customer base and stimulate sales, by all means go for it. Just make sure the return on investment is worth it.

WILL IT REDUCE COSTS?

The other very good reason. The Web can significantly reduce mailing and telephone costs. It can also reduce the need for printed material. Newsletters, product announcements, promotional literature—there are a lot of traditional paper marketing tools that can be reduced or eliminated altogether by making the same information available on your Website. Many companies are able to include enormous quantities of information on their products and services that would simply be too expensive to produce as printed materials.

If you have a product that can be distributed electronically, that can reduce costs even further. You may have a software product or printed material that can be sent to customers over the Web rather than through the mail.

WHAT ARE YOUR GOALS?

The answer to this question will determine how much money you'll need to spend in creating your site. If you're using it solely as an advertising, marketing, or customer service tool, you may find your costs lower than if you plan to sell merchandise. It really comes down to the amount of information the site contains, how often that information has to be updated, and how many bells and whistles you include.

If you have a relatively static site with just a few pages and no interactive features, your costs will be modest. Your money will largely be spent up front—selecting hardware and software and having the site designed. Once it's up it only needs the occasional updating to add new products or to reflect price changes.

If you want to check out the other end of the spectrum, spend a few days monitoring Amazon.com. It's enormous, with thousands (or even millions?) of pages. Their home page is updated daily to feature different books being sold and news on other activities of the company.

But to me the most amazing thing is the amount of links the site offers. In a big site like this, links are like cross references. The home page has links to a search tool, a browse tool, a list of the current one hundred best-sellers, a recommendation page, book reviews that appeared in the media, and other areas. Once you've purchased books from them, your name will appear as a link to a list of other titles the company is recommending based on the subject matter of your previous purchases.

When you're at a page featuring a certain book, there's a list of books purchased by people who purchased the one you're examining. If you wish, you can follow links directly to them. The author's name is linked to another page that has a list of all the author's other books. There's a link to a list of other books on the same topic, and another link that will take you to a page where you can enter your own review of the book, which other shoppers can then read. There's even a link to a page where you can enter your e-mail address so Amazon can alert you every time a new book by the same author hits the market.

Designing and maintaining a page of this size takes a veritable army of technicians. First of all, Amazon.com offers 2.5 million titles, so it's absolutely enormous. Secondly, it requires constant maintenance and updating. It also has all the bells and whistles, such as a shopping cart option and many other interactive features. It's no wonder the company required the same kind of Wall Street venture capital that's backed so many real-world technology ventures.

CAN YOU ELIMINATE THE MIDDLEMAN FROM THE PROCESS?

The Web offers companies that traditionally have sold their products through a distributor the chance to reach the end user directly. Johnston & Murphy *(http://www.johnstonmurphy.com)*, one of the nation's oldest men's shoe companies, is accomplishing this with its Website. By eliminating the retailer from the equation, they can charge their online customers a price somewhere between the wholesale and retail prices. They make a bit more money, and their customers get a break. Everybody wins.

CAN YOU BECOME A MIDDLEMAN?

Here's the flip side of the previous question. Some Web entrepreneurs have achieved success as distributors of software and specialty information on subjects such as investing and personal finance. Online directories are also quite popular.

DO YOUR CUSTOMERS WANT YOU THERE?

If they do, it's certainly a legitimate reason to investigate the move into cyberspace. Just make sure the numbers are right before taking the final step. It becomes an ''If you build it, will they come?'' question. Customers are just as prone to jumping on the Web bandwagon as businesses. But their interest may also flag. If they're not going to take advantage of what your site has to offer after you build it, you'll have wasted a lot of money.

ARE YOUR COMPETITORS THERE?

Always a good reason to enter a new market. When L.L. Bean opened its Website in 1996, all the other big mail order apparel companies were right behind them. Today they all have impressive sites with selections every bit as extensive as those offered by their catalogs.

Just make sure you don't move *too* quickly. If the other guy's making a mistake, you don't want to be diving off the cliff right behind him. Do your research to make sure there's a valid reason for both of you being on the Web. If you determine your competitor is getting a leg up on you and all your other competitors by being online, then you'll know it's the right thing to do.

WILL IT MAKE MORE PEOPLE AWARE OF YOUR PRODUCT?

Another excellent reason, *if* people can find you. This is a particular challenge for people who are starting a new business on the Web. How do you let people know you're out there? It requires careful advertising and marketing, topics we'll discuss later in the book.

CAN YOU USE YOUR SITE TO CONDUCT MARKET RESEARCH?

No question about it, one of the great things about the Web is its interactivity. You can create an online questionnaire that your customers can complete either by selecting from a multiple choice list of answers to questions about your product or service or by writing in their own answers. Not only do you get valuable information for your marketing program, you save money by not having to distribute the questionnaires by mail or conduct the survey over the phone.

CAN YOU SELL ADVERTISING TO OFFSET YOUR COSTS?

Good strategy, and one that might just work. Advertising on the Web is growing along with everything else, and if your site has the potential to generate enough traffic, it may appeal to advertisers.

CAN YOU PROVIDE BETTER CUSTOMER SERVICE?

By having frequently asked questions about products and company policy available on your Website, you can streamline your customer service efforts. Not only is it easier for them to log on to your site for information, it saves you and your employees time and effort.

You also can improve technical service by having the procedures to correct common problems on your site. Again, it makes life easier for everyone involved.

CREATING YOUR BUDGET

Now we get to the big question: How much is this going to cost?

It depends on the size of your business. If you're a small business like Jim Spitznagel's, with a limited number of products and pages, you'll probably need to spend anywhere from $2,000 to $20,000 to develop your site and conduct a marketing program during your first year online. For example, a bare-bones site with about ten pages of content and an online ordering form can be set up for about $2,500. Beyond that, price becomes a matter of size. The more pages a site has, the more expensive it will be.

A medium-sized company that wants more interactivity and may need more room for a larger product line might spend $20,000 to $50,000. This buys the equivalent of an online catalog with graphics and possibly audio and multimedia.

When we talk about high-end Websites, there are two categories: those used solely for promotion and marketing, and those used for sales. Medium- to large-sized companies that want to use their sites solely for advertising and promotion can figure on spending from $50,000 to $150,000 for a complex site that offers interactivity and anywhere from 100 to 200 pages of content. Depending on how often their pages need to be updated, they can also count on as much as $200,000 a year in maintenance.

A large company that plans to sell merchandise on the Web is going to make the most serious investment. Extensive graphics, interactive features like a shopping cart and custom-designed customer service options, transaction software, and distribution and inventory systems are expensive. If you're a firm the size of L.L. Bean, we're talking millions of dollars a year.

At first glance these figures may seem a bit scary. But look at it this way: your Website is the equivalent of a storefront. Can you imagine being able to create an entirely new venue for conducting business for less money? You're also establishing a presence in an entirely new marketplace that will hopefully provide you with more customers, improve your service, and in general contribute to a healthier bottom line.

This is not to say that success will be immediate. You may even discover you operate at a loss for a period of time. Many businesses do when they're just getting off the ground. But if you're confident in your product or service and you have a solid business plan beneath you, you can be confident in the long-term viability of your venture.

WHAT WILL YOU NEED?

Here are the basic items a small business owner will need to get an online business up and running. We'll discuss each in more detail in later chapters.

COMPUTERS

We'll start with your most important tools, your computers. For security reasons we'll explain later, you may want to have two. The first one will be connected to the Internet and used to take orders and conduct other aspects of your business. The second will be a "stand alone" machine, unconnected to all networks and the Internet, that's used to store important information like your customers' credit card numbers.

These days you have two choices when buying a computer:

an IBM-compatible machine, called a PC (personal computer), or a Macintosh. Fortunately, there are many wonderful machines out there, and they continue to get increasingly powerful while prices remain relatively stable.

The kind of computers you buy will depend on whether you want to have your site on your own computer or pay an Internet service provider to keep your site on one of its machines. These machines are called servers and are considerably more powerful than the average home computer. If you choose to use a service provider to maintain your Website, a modest home computer will serve your office purposes. (I heartily recommend this approach. We'll look at service providers in Chapter 5.) If you want your own machine to act as a server, you'll need much more memory and a more powerful and expensive machine.

Few small Web entrepreneurs have their businesses on their own computers, opting instead to use a server. It's easier and usually cheaper. Jim Spitznagel, for example, has his Website maintained by a company called Spinners, Inc., in Cambridge, Massachusetts. When customers place an order, the server in Cambridge sends the information to Jim's computer in Ithaca and he fills the order and sends the merchandise off to the customer.

Cost: $1,000 to $3,000 each

MODEM

A modem is a device that translates the data that comes over your phone lines from analog to digital and then transmits it to your computer. It then reverses the process for information you send from your computer. Many computers today have built-in modems.

Cost: $150 to $200

INTERNET ACCESS

Internet and Web access is the life link of your site. You can choose a wide range of options, from a basic connection through a service provider, which is the most inexpensive route, to a much more costly direct high-speed connection.

Cost: $90 to $1,000 per month

SOFTWARE

You'll need browser software, either Netscape Communicator or Microsoft Explorer.

Cost: $60 (or free for downloading off the Web)

YOUR DOMAIN NAME

This is your electronic name. For example, the domain name of Jim Spitznagel's compact disc business is "jims.com." Your domain name is incorporated into your URL (universal resource locator), which is the address people use to reach your site. Jim's URL is *http://www.jims.com/*.

Cost: $100 for the first two years. After two years you pay a $50-a-year retention fee.

YOUR HOST SERVER

Your host server is the company that maintains your Website. The price will depend on the size of your site and the amount of maintenance the site needs.

Cost: $50 to $500 per month

WEBSITE DEVELOPMENT

This will be one of your biggest expenses. The cost will depend on the complexity of your site and the experience of the person who designs it. As I mentioned earlier, Website design prices are all over the place.

Cost: $2,500 and up

PROMOTION

Once you're online you'll have to let people know you're there. This requires promotion and advertising.

Cost: $2,000 to $5,000

Note that all these costs are for a small business operating with a couple of computers. If you plan on having more than two computers in use, be sure to factor in the additional costs. You might also need to add in the cost of having your own "intranet" (interoffice network) established so all your computers can communicate with one another.

Note, too, that these are very rough estimates. The needs and goals of one business are going to be quite different from another. You may find that you can get started for less than the figures quoted here or it may cost you quite a bit more. The key determinants are the size and complexity of your site, the number of computers you have connected to the site, and the amount of maintenance the site requires.

Finally, these costs cover only your Website. Don't forget the overhead for your place of business (if you're lucky you'll be operating your business out of your home), utilities, inventory, printed materials, licenses, and all the other costs related to starting a business.

WHAT'S NEXT?

Now that you have some idea of what it costs to get online, you need to make decisions about hardware and software, the kind of Internet connection you need, and whether to use a server or keep your site on your own computer. There are many options with a variety of prices. We'll look at them in the next chapter.

GETTING "WIRED"

Starting a business in cyberspace requires making decisions about a lot of things you may not be very familiar with. Much as in Chapter 3, you may find a lot of the information in this chapter absolutely necessary or it may be old news.

SELECTING AN INTERNET SERVICE PROVIDER

It's time to get "wired." It's the first step in creating your online business.

Your Internet connection is the link between your computer, wherever it may be, and the Internet. You have a number of options, each offering increasing speed at increasing prices. The least expensive—and slowest—connections will link you through your phone jack and the same copper wires used by the telephone companies. It might cost as little as $20 a month. At the other end of the spectrum are several state-of-the-art connections that provide lightning-fast data transfer at premium prices.

Whatever kind of connection you choose, you're going to have to obtain it through an Internet Service Provider (ISP). The following questions will determine which one you choose.

WHERE WILL YOUR WEBSITE "LIVE"?

This might be your biggest consideration in selecting an ISP. Your Website needs a home—a host computer that's accessible to your customers twenty-four hours a day, 365 days a year. The computer that houses your Website is called a "server."

You have three options, two of which we'll discuss through the rest of the chapter. The first is to have your ISP maintain your site on one of its servers along with the Websites of other businesses and organizations. The second is to have your own dedicated server— one that's reserved exclusively for your use—at your ISP's facility.

The third option is to maintain your Website on your own server. This means you'll be responsible for maintaining your site, a headache you really don't need if you're trying to run a business. It's also usually extremely expensive. Most online businesses that do maintain their own servers are large enough to require networks of servers and a number of full-time, well-paid technicians to babysit them. This isn't to say there aren't some business owners in cyberspace who maintain their own servers. There are. But if they do, they have enough technical expertise that they don't need to read books like this.

For small business owners, the easiest option is to have your ISP keep your site on one of its computers with other Websites. When you do this, you're "renting" memory on the machine's hard drive, much as you'd rent a storefront for a conventional business. The more memory you need, the more you pay each month. If your site is large enough and has enough traffic, you may need to have your own dedicated server.

But there's more to it than that. Unless you're particularly skilled in the language of the Web and have a lot of time on your hands, you're going to want your ISP to be in charge of maintaining your site—updating information, adding new pages, deleting outdated information, and the like. This requires technical skills that not all ISPs are prepared to offer.

DOES THE ISP OFFER ALL THE SERVICES YOU NEED?

Before you start shopping around for an ISP, you'll need a list of the services you're going to need to operate your business. At the very least, you'll want the following.

• A PPP (point-to-point protocol) account. This gives you direct access to the Internet. If the service provider can

only offer a SLIP account or a Shell account, look elsewhere. Both are inferior and outdated technologies.

- World Wide Web access.
- At least one e-mail account.
- FTP (file transfer protocol), which allows you to send and
  receive files of data.
- Usenet, the conglomeration of discussion groups I men-
  tioned earlier in the book.

WHAT'S THE SPEED OF THE ISP'S INTERNET CONNECTION(S)?

They should have a minimum of two T-1 lines, each of which
should be connected to a different "backbone" (this is the line
that provides the T-1 connection to the ISP). That way, if one
connection goes down, they can operate through the second. If
they have faster connections, that's even better.

HOW LONG HAVE THEY BEEN OFFERING INTERNET SERVICE?

This is extremely important. Like any new industry, the rapid
growth of the Internet and the Web has generated thousands of
related businesses. Some are great. Others are in way over their
heads and are basically flying by the seat of their pants and
learning as they go along. Let them learn with other people.
You have a business to run. If the company is less than two
years old, look elsewhere.

WHAT KIND OF CONNECTIONS DO THEY OFFER AND WHAT'S THE HIGHEST SPEED OF EACH?

They should have a range of options. This will allow you to
upgrade later if business demands it without having to switch
to a new ISP.

DO THEY HAVE ROUND-THE-CLOCK STAFFING?

You want twenty-four hour a day access, which means someone
has to be there at all times to fix problems.

WHAT HARDWARE AND SOFTWARE ARE INCLUDED IN THEIR PRICES?

Don't expect much in the way of hardware, but they should provide all the software to meet your needs. Even then, find out how old it is. In the world of the Internet and the Web, today's state-of-the-art software is tomorrow's Model T.

WHAT IS THEIR CUSTOMER-TO-MODEM RATIO?

How many other customers are you sharing your connectivity with? Look for ten or less.

HOW FAST A CONNECTION DO YOU NEED?

The answer to this is simple. You need the fastest connection you can afford. Here are your choices.

OPTION #1: USE A "DIAL-UP" SERVICE

Your first and usually most affordable option is to use a commercial service that connects you to the Internet through your telephone line. The most familiar names are the large nationwide companies like America Online, Prodigy, and CompuServe. These were among the earliest companies to take advantage of the Web, but they only used it to make content that they developed available to their customers. They didn't offer full access to the Web. Now they do, thanks to the entry of hundreds of smaller regional service providers into the market.

While these large online services are certainly viable choices, they're expensive as well, charging businesses a percentage of their revenues and additional online advertising fees. Chances are you can get equally reliable service from a local or regional provider. There are more than ever these days. To find one, just look in the yellow pages of your phone book, check the ads in your newspaper, or log on to the Websites listed at the end of this chapter.

Dial-up Internet connections usually cost about $20 a month.

You may have to pay a bit more for a business connection. Some companies will charge you a flat rate. Others may have a sliding scale based on how often you use the service.

To use a dial-up connection, you'll need a modem, which translates the data that comes across your phone line and transmits it to your computer. Some computers have built-in modems. Others are external and connect to your computer with a short cable.

The speed with which your computer receives data will be determined by the speed of your modem. The fastest modems today are able to transmit at 56 kbps (kilobytes per second, or 56,000 bits per second). That's much faster than modems of just two years ago but much slower than some other options we'll examine. Still, for most small businesses, a dial-up connection with a 56 kbps modem is perfectly adequate.

Even if you use a local provider, it might not be a bad idea to have a second connection through one of the larger online services. For one thing, it can serve as a backup if your local provider has a problem. It can also connect you to millions of other subscribers. It's well worth the extra $20 it might cost you each month.

OPTION #2: GET AN ISDN LINE

An ISDN (Integrated Services Digital Network) line is a faster connection. It's also much more expensive. You have two choices of speeds: 56/64 kbps (one channel) or 112/128 kbps (two channels).

ISDN is being offered by some ISPs and by many phone companies. Like dial-up access, it uses regular telephone lines. But it's completely digital, which means you won't need a modem. You will, however, need an expensive network terminal adapter. If you have two or more computers connected to each other, you'll need an even more expensive routing device.

The pros of ISDN connections are the speed and the instant access they provide to the Internet and Web. Another advantage is that you can use a single line for more than one function at a time. You can make phone calls, send faxes, and be on the Web all at once.

The obvious downside is the cost—from $500 to $2,000 for installation and hardware, a $50 monthly fee, and charges from the phone company for every second you're on the line. Even though it's only a few pennies per minute, the charges can really add up over a month.

Option #3: Get a Digital Subscriber Line

I mentioned one part of this technology, the asymmetrical digital subscriber line (ADSL), in Chapter 1. That's the one being worked on by the big consortium of computer and telephone companies and, with its 1.5 million bytes-per-second speed and ability to be delivered over telephone lines, touted as the first national standard. However, there are several other slower versions of DSL that are currently available in some metropolitan regions.

Existing DSL connections offer speeds as high as 768 kbps. Data is delivered over regular copper telephone wires but, oddly enough, it doesn't have the capability to carry voice. Things are still somewhat in the experimental stage, so quoting prices is difficult. But depending on the speed of the connection, DSL service might run anywhere from $100 to $200 a month.

Option #4: Use Cable Access

Obtaining your Internet connection through your cable provider will also give you blazing speed. More and more cable television companies are providing this service, for installation charges of $100 or so and monthly fees of $40 to $50. What a lot of them are not doing, however, is offering Website host services. This means if you use a cable company for Internet access, you'll probably need to use another ISP to house your Website.

Option #5: Get a Network Connection

This is really getting wired. A network connection is the fastest—and most expensive—toy out there. We're talking serious data transmission via the three fastest tools on the Internet: T-1,

T-2, and T-3 lines. These use fiber optic cables that send bits and bytes whizzing around at literally the speed of light.

We're also talking serious money, so unless you have a huge company the size of L.L. Bean or Amazon.com, and a budget to match, this type of network will probably be a bit out of reach. A complete T-1 line service, and its 1.5 mbps speed, can cost as much as $2,000 a month, with another $3,000 needed to install it. Sharing a T-3 line (the fastest of the three at 45 mbps) to achieve 4 mbps speed might cost $7,000 a month with a $7,500 installation fee. This is clearly the realm of the big boys.

SELECTING A WEBSITE HOST

If you follow my recommendation and have your ISP house and maintain your Website, you'll have a whole new list of considerations to deal with.

Your first task will be to determine what sort of server arrangement you need. You can share a server with other Web businesses (the thriftiest option) or you can have a server (or a number of servers) devoted solely to your site (increasingly expensive options).

Your decision will be governed by the size of your site. Most small businesses make out just fine sharing a server with other businesses and organizations. Traffic to their sites is modest enough that access doesn't become an issue and all the residents on the server manage to carry out their activities without getting in one another's way. Many servers will host several dozen Websites without any problems.

But for businesses that have many pages, tons of graphics, multimedia presentations, and lots of visitors, a dedicated server for their own use may be the only option. Sites the size of Amazon.com and L.L. Bean require networks of dedicated servers to handle the enormous number of pages they maintain and the tens of thousands of customers they have every day.

Some companies deal with the volume issue by having mirror sites. These are servers located around the country, each of which is responsible for handling business within a specific geographic region.

How Expensive Are They?

As I mentioned before, the cheaper option is to keep your site on one of your ISP's servers. You'll have no costs for hardware or software. You'll pay anywhere from $50 to $200 for installation. Your monthly fee will be from $20 to $500, depending on how much memory you need and how active the site is. And annual maintenance fees will run from $500 to $5,000, depending on how often the information on your site has to be updated.

A dedicated server gets much more expensive. You'll probably be responsible for providing hardware and software, which can be as much as $6,000. Installation charges can reach $2,000. Monthly fees will range from $250 to $5,000, again depending on traffic. And site maintenance can be anywhere from $5,000 to $50,000 or more.

WHAT QUESTIONS SHOULD YOU ASK?

In addition to the ISP questions I outlined earlier in the chapter, you'll need to ask the following questions of your Website host.

Do They Provide Round-the-Clock Technical Support?

If your host server goes down, you're out of business until the problem is fixed. If this happens in the middle of the night, you don't want to have to wait until someone comes waltzing in at nine A.M. before you're back online.

What Percentage of the ISP's Connection Capacity Is Used?

The answer to this question will determine your risk of suffering a slowed connection. When connection capacity, or "system load," reaches around 50 percent, performance begins to fall off rapidly. If it approaches 100 percent, the connection can come to a complete stop.

WHAT KIND OF MACHINE WILL HOUSE YOUR WEBSITE?

The faster the processing speed, the faster your Web pages will be delivered to your customers. Macintosh OS machines with Power PC chips are adequate, as are Pentium-class PCs with 150 megahertz (Mhz) speed. Anything faster is even better.

HOW MANY SITES WILL SHARE YOUR SERVER?

This is not a case of "the more, the merrier." If a server is too crowded, it will slow the delivery of pages to your customers. This is lousy customer service and must be avoided at all costs. If a site is too slow to download, customers won't hang around.

DO THEY HAVE A SECURE SERVER?

If you're going to be taking credit card orders, you're going to need one.

DO THEY HAVE A BACKUP SYSTEM?

In the computer world, there's one word that's feared more than any other: *crash!* If it happens to your server and the ISP hasn't backed up (stored all the data from that server on a backup server) you're dead in the water. Backup should be done at least once a week.

DO THEY HAVE THE TECHNICAL EXPERTISE YOU NEED?

You're going to be relying on your ISP to maintain your pages. You may also prefer one that offers Web design services. Down the road you may want to add a shopping cart feature or other customer service features. If business is booming, you may even want to expand your site. Make sure the ISP has the technical expertise to do these things for you.

What Do They Expect You to Do?

Turn the questioning around and ask them what they expect from their clients. This is a good way to make sure there aren't any minor details being missed. It also will let you know if there are any tasks that you're uncomfortable with. If there are, their execution can be negotiated or you can look for another service provider.

Ask For References

Always a good strategy. Talk to other business people who use their service. If there are concerns, you'll soon find out what they are.

PROBLEMS TO WATCH OUT FOR

As you go through the above steps in selecting an ISP/Website host, watch out for the following.

Transaction-Based Fees

Some ISPs will hit you with a charge every time you carry out a certain transaction. Among the most objectionable are credit card transaction fees and e-mail fees. If you have to pay five or ten cents every time you receive a credit card order or send or receive an e-mail message, the total bill at the end of the month can be outrageous. E-mail charges are especially vexing, since sending one e-mail message costs the ISP the same amount as sending a hundred messages.

Unreasonable Charges

Many ISPs are taking advantage of new subscribers' lack of knowledge and charging them for everything imaginable. You can avoid this by comparison shopping. Look carefully at a half-dozen or more ISPs and compare prices for different services before you make a decision on which to use.

OVERSTUFFED PHONE LINES

Any business that uses a modem to connect to its ISP needs to make sure its phone company doesn't have them on a Digital Added Main Line (DAML, rhymes with "camel"). This is a line that stuffs two phone lines into the wires meant to support one. It's a common solution to the problems caused by running short of phone lines in a neighborhood. Although it doesn't affect voice transmission, it will cut the speed of your modem in half.

LONG-DISTANCE CHARGES

This is frequently a big problem for people who use modems and have their connection through one of the national service providers. You may be hit with a long-distance charge every time you use the Internet.

LONG-TERM CONTRACTS

Some Internet service providers may offer you a discount if you sign a long-term service contract. Don't do it. Go month-to-month only. Your Internet connection is the only artery between you and your customers. If you're unhappy with your service, you need to be able to bail out and switch to a new ISP without losing money.

DISCLAIMERS

Some ISPs will include a disclaimer in their service contracts absolving them of any responsibility if your service should not be up to snuff. That's ridiculous. If you have an ISDN or faster connection, your contract should specify the maximum time it should take for data to reach you from your provider.

CLAIMS ON TRANSMITTED MATERIAL

There have also been instances where ISPs will include a contract clause claiming the rights to information, software, or any

other data that moves through their service from your business.
No way. The exact opposite should be stated. The ISP should
have no rights to any information related to the operation of
your business.

SELECTING YOUR COMPUTERS, MODEM, AND OTHER EQUIPMENT

Even though you're conducting business in cyberspace, you're
still going to have a lot of real-world tasks. These will require
the same equipment all offices use these days. Each piece of
equipment you already own is one less item that will have to
be included in your budget.

COMPUTERS

Hopefully, you already have computers that are adequate for
your business. If you don't, as I pointed out in Chapter 4,
you can either get PC compatible machines or Macintoshes.
Personally, I favor Macs. I find them much easier to use than
PCs. Their operating systems are thought out in a very logical
manner, so if you don't know how to do something, you can
usually figure it out. We use Macs in my office, and my wife
and I each have our own machines at home.

But PCs have always made up the majority of the market.
And even I, a diehard Mac fan, have to admit they're becoming
more pleasant to use, largely due to improved software such as
Microsoft's Windows. There is also tons more software available for PCs than for Macs.

Whichever you choose, you can be confident you're getting
a lot for your money. The computer is one of the few consumer
products that keeps getting better and better while prices remain
fairly static. Both hard drive memory and RAM—random access memory, that portion of the machine's memory that you
can use to do a variety of tasks—keep increasing. Processor
speed keeps getting faster. And added features such as CD-
ROM capability keep getting better and more numerous.

Since you're going to be using an outside server, your computers are going to need far less memory than if you had decided to maintain your site yourself. You'll be using one of your machines to receive orders, which will be sent to you via e-mail, as well as other "office" tasks—billing, correspondence, etc. Your second machine will be used solely to store confidential data. If you buy PCs, you should have at least Pentium or 586 class machines with Windows 95 or later as an operating system. If you buy Macintoshes, you'll need a Power Mac with a 7.5 or later operating system. Both machines should have at least 32 megabytes of RAM. If you need to, you can have additional RAM installed by the dealer who sells you your machines.

MONITOR

Here's another helpful hint. Invest in a large color monitor, at least 19 inches. You can open many more documents on your desktop and make them much larger than you can with a 13- or 14-inch monitor. I work on a 19-inch monitor at my office and a 13-incher at home, and believe me, there's a world of difference.

MODEM

If you're going to use dial-up access for your Internet connection, you'll need a modem. Buy the fastest modem you can get, currently 56 kbps. One word of warning, though. Before you invest in a modem, make sure your service provider can transmit at that speed. There's no point in shelling out money for technology you're unable to use.

You can also purchase a computer with a built-in modem. These are becoming more common every year.

TELEPHONE

This is another real-world tool you can't do without. Although the Internet and e-mail have reduced the amount of time most people spend on the phone, they haven't replaced it altogether. First of all, not everyone you'll need to deal with in your business is going to have e-mail. And even if they do, there are going to be times when the only way to really accomplish what you need to accomplish is over the phone. For example, what will you do when your Internet connection (and therefore your e-mail) suddenly goes down and you need to contact your ISP? Send a telegram?

Like any business, you'll no doubt have to keep track of many phone numbers. Many models today allow you to load a dozen or more numbers into the phone's memory, enabling you to dial frequently called numbers with the push of a button. If you anticipate juggling a lot of calls at one time, you may need a hold button. Telephone headsets are also available that allow you to keep both hands free to take notes or accomplish other tasks. Cellular phones are also very convenient, although you run the risk of other people accidentally overhearing your conversations.

The phone company will also offer options you may want to consider. Call waiting is usually a valuable and inexpensive investment. Other custom calling features include caller ID (to let you know who's calling), call forwarding, conference calling for business meetings held over the phone, and voice mail messaging.

You'll Need More Than One Telephone Line

Your phone connection will channel much more than just voice communication into your office. It also will connect your fax machine and your modem and computer. For this reason you should have a separate line for each piece of equipment. If you don't, the use of one piece of equipment will preclude the use of the others. You can also buy a switcher that will automatically route each incoming call to the phone, the fax, or the computer.

Should You Get a Toll-Free Number?

Yes. It's absolutely essential to good customer service. Remember, some of your customers won't be comfortable sending credit card information over the Web. And all your customers may want to contact you with questions about your products. You need to absorb the costs of these communications. Although a toll call isn't going to break anybody's budget, if your customers have to spend their own money to order merchandise or get information, it will definitely leave a bad taste in their mouths. It could prevent them from doing business with you altogether.

ANSWERING MACHINE

If you include your phone number anywhere in your business information, whether in printed material, advertising, or on your Website, you'll need an answering machine. No business can afford poor customer relations, and there's nothing more aggravating to a customer than calling a business and not getting an answer. So an answering machine is fairly inexpensive insurance against unhappy customers. You can buy one for less than $100. Keep your message short and businesslike, remember to check your messages every time you return to the office, and return calls as soon as possible.

FAX MACHINE

As fax machines have come down in price, they've become an invaluable tool for small businesses. Even though you'll have e-mail and a telephone, a fax machine is a must. The most important reason to have one is to service those customers who aren't comfortable sending their credit card numbers over the Internet. One option you'll include on your Website is an order form that can be printed out and either faxed to you or sent in the mail.

Fax machines come with a wide variety of features and in a wide variety of prices. Basic features include line in/line out, an automatic paper cutter, automatic transmission, and a multipage document feeder. Beyond that you'll need to determine what special features you'll need. One I've found useful for those times when the receiving machine is busy is the automatic call back. This allows you to go about your business while your machine automatically redials the receiving machine until it gets through. When it does, it feeds your document through the scanner and sends it on its way. Some machines have memory features that allow you to scan a document and have it sent later, or resend it over and over until it's received.

Before buying a fax machine, check out its image quality by sending a few test documents. Many faxes still use thermal paper, which tends to fade and wrinkle over time. There are faxes available that use plain paper but they're still quite pricey. You can also buy machines that function as a fax, a copier, and a printer for your computer, but again, they may be priced out of your reach. Don't feel too covetous of them. Generally they are barely adequate and quite slow as printers and copiers.

If you prefer to take care of your fax needs with your computer, you might want to buy a fax/modem. This will allow you to send faxes of documents right from your computer, eliminating the need for hard copy. Be aware, however, that computers receive faxes as graphic documents, not text documents. That means they take up a lot of hard disk space and can't be edited.

PRINTER

Like any other business, you'll need a printer to create invoices, correspondence, order forms, spread sheets, and all the other documents you'll create on your computer.

The simplest and cheapest printers are dot matrix. Mid-priced printers use a thermal ink jet technology, and the best printers are laser printers. When you're comparing different printers, consider the speed with which they print, the visual quality of the documents, and the expense of the ink or toner cartridges. Also, make sure the documents don't smear.

Like computers, printer technology is continually improving. My recommendation is a thermal ink jet printer, which you can buy for less than $300. I've been using one for several years and have been more than happy with it. It produces quality documents and it's relatively fast.

SOFTWARE

Software is what makes the computer do the things you want it to do. Just as there are basic tools that should be found in every office, there are basic software programs that should be included in every business computer. Depending on your needs, you can augment them with additional programs.

Your two biggest needs will be a word-processing program for correspondence and a basic financial management program to keep track of your financial information. A data-base program will also be useful to keep records of customers, projects, and other information.

There are many programs on the market that can accomplish these tasks. Some—Claris Works comes to mind because it came preloaded on my Mac—include these types of programs plus several others "bundled" in a single package. Like Apple, many computer manufacturers are including this type of software for free as a marketing tool, so the chances are the computer you buy will already have the basic software you'll need. Once you have the basics, you can augment them with other programs that serve your needs.

SELECTING YOUR DOMAIN NAME

There are two languages spoken in cyberspace. One is the language computers use to communicate with each other. The second is the language that humans use to communicate with computers.

This is where domain names come into play. A domain name is a term such as "sears.com" that identifies your Website to users. The first word usually is associated with your business. The second word, "com," denotes the fact that it is a commercial enterprise. Your domain name then becomes incorporated into your URL (universal resource locator), which is your complete Web address. For example, Sears Roebuck's URL is *http://www.sears.com.*

Domain names have been assigned to circumvent the way computers refer to each other. Every computer on the Internet is assigned a unique number, such as 157.5.95.38. While this system works just fine for computers when they want to locate each other, it's a nightmare for people. I can rattle off the addresses of dozens of Websites from memory simply because of their domain names. It's unlikely that I'd be able to do the same if I had to remember their numbers.

U.S. Registration Agencies

There are two agencies in the United States authorized to register user-selected domain names under what are referred to as "top-level domains." The first is the InterNIC *(http://rs.internic. net/index.html)*, which is operated by Network Solutions Registration Services, Inc. under contract to the National Science Foundation. The second is the U.S. Domain Registry *(www. isi.edu:80/in-notes/usdnr/)*.

The problem for users is that each of these registries uses a different syntax in making up its names. The InterNIC, for example, can assign six top-level domains that indicate the nature of the applicant's activities and appear at the end of their URLs. They are:

.com—assigned to commercial enterprises
.edu—assigned to educational institutions
.org—assigned to not-for-profit organizations
.gov—assigned to government agencies
.mil—assigned to military organizations
.net—usually reserved for Internet service providers

The InterNIC can also assign "second-level domains" such as "sears." To complete the URL, your service provider will add a machine name, typically "www," to complete the full Web address *http://www.sears.com.* (Actually, the *http://* is no longer necessary with most browsers. It's become a given and the browsers will "assume" that it's part of the address.)

All U.S. Domain Registry (USDR) domain names, on the other hand, end in ".us" and include second-, third-, and fourth-level domain names based on geographic location. For example, Sears Roebuck's domain name, if obtained through the USDR, would be something like *sears.chicago.ill.us.* This system gets a bit cumbersome and does not lend itself to intuitively finding a business on the Web.

To streamline the domain name issue, it's expected that many more top-level domains may eventually be added, such as .food, .music, .law, .sports, etc. This would allow greater diversity in assigning domain names and would also eliminate the very real problem of running short of domain names altogether.

It would also help eliminate confusion between companies that have the same name but aren't in competition with each other. If, for example, fledgling Web entrepreneur Irving B. Martin wanted to start an online business selling golf clubs and to use his initials as his domain name, he might actually be able to do it using the name "ibm.golf." As you can probably guess, "ibm.com" is already taken by a rather large and well-known computer company.

On the other hand, he might be out of luck. A lot of big companies have registered all sorts of variations of their names simply to protect themselves, so there's no guarantee that Big Blue won't have beaten him to the punch and already registered "ibm.golf." You can bet they'll be scrambling to register other ibm domain names. Each one would only cost them a hundred bucks. They can afford it.

How Do You Apply for Your Domain Name?

It's simple. You apply to one of the two registry agencies. You can do this online, but it has to be done through a service provider in order for the domain name to be registered to a specific computer.

The InterNIC limits domain names to twenty-six characters, including the "dot" and the three-letter top-level domain. It charges a fee of $100, which makes the name valid for two years. After that you must pay a $50 annual fee to continue to use the name. If you let your registration lapse, your domain name can be reassigned. The USDR does not charge a fee to register domain names, but your service provider may charge you a small fee for its service.

What Domain Name Should You Choose?

Selecting the proper domain name is critical to making your site accessible. The most obvious choice for a domain name is your business name. Because of the enormous number of domain names that have already been registered over the last five years, however, there's a good chance it will have already been taken. Domain names are like license plate numbers. Each one can only be used once. A look at the explosive increase in the number of registrations in the last few years will give you an idea of how many names have already been taken. In 1992, when Network Solutions was first awarded its contract, it registered approximately 7,500 names. In 1996, it registered 489,000. In 1997, 960,000.

If your first choice has been taken, a variation of your name or product is the next best option. You should have several names selected before you begin the registration process in case your first choice is already taken.

You do have one more option. You can buy the name you want to use from the person or company who beat you to it. There are many precedents for this. In 1997, for example, a company in Texas paid $150,000 to Business Systems International of London for the rights to "business.com."

There are also a number of stories about people who had the foresight to register the names of some of the nation's largest corporations early on. Then when these companies wanted to set up Websites, they had to buy the rights to use their own names. At least one big corporate name, coke.com, is still registered to an individual, Rajeev Arora, who lives in California. As you can imagine, this practice has raised all sorts of thorny legal questions involving trademarks and is being carefully examined.

Can You Check to See What Names Are Already Taken?

Yes, it's easy. All you have to do is go to the InterNIC's "whois" page (*http://rs.internic.net/cgi-bin/whois*). You'll see a dialogue box in which you type the domain name you've selected, including ".com," and press the return key on your keyboard. If the domain name is already being used, you'll get a reply telling you who has it. If the name is available, the search will tell you it found no match for the name you submitted.

To see how this works, I conducted a little experiment while writing this book. I pretended I wanted to start a compact disc business like Jim Spitznagel's and decided my first choice for a domain name would be ''mikes.com.'' A quick check with the InterNIC, however, showed me that ''mikes.com'' had already been registered by Mike's Motor Company, a Chrysler/ Jeep dealership in Clinton, Indiana.

So then I started thinking of alternatives. My first idea was to remove the letter *s* from ''mikes'' and try ''mike.com.'' Late again. This one is registered by Inresco Portfolios Ltd. in Etna, New Hampshire. But on my next try, ''mikesmusic.com,'' I hit paydirt. That domain name had not been registered and was mine if I wanted it.

Just out of curiosity, I then conducted a random search of domain names to see what else had been taken. I made some interesting discoveries: ''shoebox.com'' is registered to Hallmark Cards, Inc.; ''matterhorn.com'' belongs to Valhalla USA in Oakland, California; ''speedtrap.com'' is the property of WWW Speedtrap Registry in Nashville, Tennessee; and ''beer. com'' is held by the Bilfish Energy Exchange Reserve in Denver.

Okay, these are relatively common terms, I thought to myself. Let's see what happens when I get really silly and try names no one would ever use. Well, was I ever surprised. My first attempt, ''nosehair.com,'' turned out to be registered to International Systems Research Co. in Chicago. Then I tried ''wood chuck.com,'' which has been claimed by the Stroh's Brewery in Detroit. I thought I had a winner with ''greaseball.com,'' but no such luck. That one's the property of Internet Domains in Huntington Beach, California. Even ''pothead.com'' has been taken. It was registered by Happy Dicks Productions in Marietta, Georgia.

WHY AREN'T ALL REGISTERED DOMAIN NAMES BEING USED?

One interesting note to all this. Just because a domain name has been registered doesn't mean that a Website has been created using that name. Attempts to find sites using the above domain names almost always ended with my browser telling me it was unable to locate a server. The exceptions were the "shoebox" site, which is the Website of Hallmark's Shoebox division; the Stroh's "woodchuck" site, which turned out to be the home page of the Green Mountain Cidery, makers of Woodchuck Draft Cider; and the "speedtrap" site, which is a comprehensive directory of speedtraps both in the United States and overseas that's maintained by a Vanderbilt University computer science major.

Why have the other domain names been registered? They're either highly speculative investments made by companies and individuals who registered large numbers of names in the hope they'd be able to sell them down the road to businesses who want to use them for their Websites, or they were registered by companies that wanted to protect names they thought they might use themselves someday. Kraft Foods, for example, registered 132 domain names in 1995.

But don't forget, anything can be had for the right price. If you have a business that sells tweezers and you think "nose hair.com" might be the perfect domain name for your Website, call International Systems Research Co. at 312-871-3471 and ask for Brian. Maybe the two of you can work out a deal.

CREATING A TIMELINE

Like any business, your Web business will require a timeline to help you plan and accomplish the various tasks involved and set a deadline for launching your Website. Although there's certainly no prescribed time period for accomplishing this, we'll use a twenty-one-week time frame. The amount of time you need will be determined by the size and complexity of your business.

Time frame	Tasks to be Accomplished
Weeks 1–4	Sketch out the mission and goals of your business. What products or services will you sell? Who are your customers? How will doing business on the Web help you meet your goals? Determine equipment needs.

Weeks 5–6	Contact and research ISPs to help you determine what kind of Internet connection you need and which ISP will host your Website. Establish prices for all the services you'll need.
Weeks 7–8	Contact and research Website designers. Sketch out rough structure for your site. Establish prices for all the services you'll need.
Weeks 9–10	Review information and proposals from ISPs and Web designers. Make selections and contract for services. Create budget and business plan.
Week 11	Purchase computer, modem, fax machine, printer, and other needed equipment. Arrange for installation of all equipment and Internet connections.
Weeks 12–13	Begin work on Website with Web designer. Begin planning both online and conventional advertising and PR strategies.
Weeks 14–18	Continue Web development and PR planning. Establish procedures for receiving and filling orders, providing various customer services, and other personal business responsibilities. Begin advertising and PR campaign.
Weeks 19–20	Finish Website and make final preparations to begin business.
Week 21	Launch Website.

WHAT'S NEXT?

This chapter has helped you create the skeleton of your Web business. Now it's time to create the heart—the Website itself. In Chapter 6 we'll examine what constitutes an efficient and well-designed site and how you can find someone to design yours.

FOR MORE INFORMATION

Here are some sites that can give you more information on Internet service providers and other topics.

➡ **AT&T WorldNet** (*http://www.att.com/worldnet*) AT&T has offered direct Internet access since early 1996. This site includes information on their services, pricing, and sign-up.

➡ **IBM Global Services** (*http://www.ibm.com/globalnetwork*) IBM also offers Internet access. Big Blue's site provides a description of its services, prices, and local access numbers.

➡ **POCIA** (Providers of Commercial Internet Access) (*http://www.celestin.com/pocia/index.html*) This site offers a collection of links to nearly one thousand Internet service providers, including many who provide Website hosting.

➡ **The List** (*http://thelist.internet.com/*) It's just what it says it is, a list of about 6,400 service providers and a search directory to help you find the ones closest to you.

BUILDING YOUR WEBSITE

I can't stress enough the importance of the structure and design of your Website. Its appearance, its organization, and the ease with which people can move about your site are every bit as important to the success of your business as your product or service.

This is because your Website is the online equivalent of your office or storefront. If you already have a conventional store, you no doubt go out of your way to make it inviting to your customers. You make it as attractive as possible from the outside—colorful, clean, and well-lit—with intriguing items in your windows. I'm sure even more attention is paid to the interior, with merchandise well-organized and neatly arranged and your best items highlighted with special displays.

You're also concerned about customer service and would be horrified that someone might walk out your door because they hadn't been approached by a salesperson to see if they needed any help or had a question to which they couldn't find an answer.

All these concerns are equally important to businesses on the Web. We'll start with your home page. This is the first thing customers see when they visit your site, so think of it as your storefront. It needs to be well-designed, provide clear information on what customers will find in your site, and then entice them to click their way in. Once they've entered, it's just as if they've walked through the door of your store. They need to be able to find their way around and view your merchandise without difficulty. If they have questions, they need to receive answers. And when they're ready to make a purchase, the process should be as simple and quick as possible.

If your cybercustomers don't find these qualities in your site, they'll do just what customers do in the physical world—find some other place to shop. If they do, you'll quickly be out of business. This chapter will help you make your online store as exciting and customer-friendly as possible.

CHOOSING A WEB DESIGNER

I think I just made my case for why the design of your Website is no job for amateurs. You need to find the best and most experienced designer you can. It's not just for aesthetic reasons, although the appearance of your site is certainly very important. It's also because of all the other concerns that go into making a site useful. Good Website designers are part artist, part technician, part psychologist, part linguist, part cartographer, and part tour guide, mixed with healthy portions of plain old computer geek. In short, they really have to know what they're doing in a whole lot of areas.

Despite this fact, some people attempt to design their sites themselves. Can you do it yourself? The answer, and I say this reluctantly, is yes, provided you have the complete set of tools needed to create a sophisticated and user-friendly site. The key word here is complete. A lot of people run out to a class to learn the basics of HTML, buy themselves a scanner, and decide they're ready to start designing Web pages. The truth of the matter is they're really only ready to put some words and pictures on the Web. As I mentioned before, a good Website is much more than that. My advice is to hire an expert, no matter how much Web experience you've had.

Another common mistake people make is hiring people who, although they may have some Web training, either haven't designed anything more complex than a personal Website or have never designed a site for a business. Many businesses make the mistake of assigning the task to their designated computer guru, the person who, whether through training or personal interest, has developed the expertise needed to take care of the business's computer operations. Unless these people are inordinately talented, the results usually show it.

HIRE AN EXPERT

Having your Website designed is not the place to cut corners. You need somebody with experience, who keeps up with the technology, who has created sites for other businesses, and who can show you a portfolio of a half-dozen or more sites. Having your site designed is a critical part of your business and should be carried out with the utmost care. Take your time, ask as many questions of your candidates as possible, and carefully evaluate their work on other Websites. Here are some of the questions you'll want answered:

HOW MANY YEARS HAS THE DESIGNER BEEN IN BUSINESS?

Like every other aspect of life on the Web, there are people with all sorts of backgrounds offering Web design services. Some are trained graphic designers who have made the transition to designing electronically and are able to create wondrous—if not always practical—sites. Others are people with years of computer experience who have decided that Web page design is just one more facet of the work they've been doing. As with other new computer tasks, they figure that taking a few classes and reading a few tutorials will provide them with everything they need to know.

They couldn't be more wrong. Website design requires a whole new way of thinking. The appearance of a page is just one consideration. But there are many others. For example, how long does it take the page to download? The more graphics files and HTML files it contains, the longer it will take to arrive on a customer's monitor. If it takes too long to download, your customer will go elsewhere. Remember what we learned in Chapter 2. Studies of Web shoppers have shown that slow speed is the most commonly cited problem with online shopping, and seven out of ten experienced Web users report losing patience and leaving a site before completing a transaction.

Another issue is user-friendliness. How easy is it to navigate from one page to another in the site? A poorly designed site can quickly leave a visitor feeling lost and, once again, result in them hitting the digital pavement in search of a better place to shop.

The designer you select should have at least two years' experience designing Websites. And look at all the work they've done. Make sure they've had experience creating all the features you'll want your site to have. In the end, that will really be a deciding factor in who you choose to work with.

Do You and the Designer Share a Design Philosophy?

This is another deciding factor. If you want spare and simple and your designer comes up with big and gaudy, you're not going to be very happy.

Does the Designer Take Responsibility for Creating All the Components of the Website or Are Some of Them Contracted to Others?

If the designer does sub out some of the work, this creates a whole new set of folks you need to investigate. While this isn't necessarily a reason not to hire someone, it does create more work for you. But it's probably worth the trouble if the work they've done is good and the price is right.

Does the Designer Host Websites as Well as Create Them?

If so, what other services does he or she offer? Frankly, the most convenient path in all this is to find an ISP who offers knockout Website design services as well as site hosting and maintenance. It's one-stop shopping and will make your life considerably easier.

HAS THE DESIGNER CREATED WEBSITES WITH A SHOPPING CART FEATURE?

Shopping cart features make online shopping extremely simple and are quickly becoming a standard part of Web businesses of all sizes. They're simple to use. On each page that describes a piece of merchandise, there will be a button that says something like "add to shopping cart." If you want to buy the item, you click the button and the item is added to a list of other items you've selected.

When you've selected all the items you want to buy, you hit another button that says "proceed to checkout." This takes you to a final page where you can review the items in your shopping cart, delete any you decide you don't really want, and then enter your name, address, and credit card number on the electronic order form. You hit one final "send order" button and your order is on its way.

I think a shopping cart feature is a must for any business selling merchandise on the Web. It's the ultimate in ease and speed and makes the whole process extremely simple for your customers.

HAS THE DESIGNER CREATED WEBSITES WITH VIDEO, AUDIO, OR MULTIMEDIA?

These are features you probably won't need, at least not at first. The expense involved usually makes them prohibitive for small businesses. But what happens if business is good and your site expands? You may want to add them down the road. If your designer has had experience designing these features, it will save you the trouble of looking for a new designer to add them.

HAS THE DESIGNER CREATED DATA BASE WEBSITES THAT CREATE PAGES ON DEMAND?

Rather than having pages designed and ready to open, a data base Website uses a template to create a page when the page is requested. The template has predetermined locations for various kinds of information. When a request is made to see the page, the program pulls the information from the appropriate data bases and creates an instant page.

This is a feature used by businesses such as Amazon.com that require tens of thousands of pages to hawk their wares. The company carries more than 2.5 million titles, and you can visit a page for each one. Obviously, it would be prohibitively expensive and time consuming to have a separate page for each one sitting on the company's servers. Data-base design technology offers a shortcut that makes it possible for companies this size to present all their items, no matter how numerous they may be.

It's unlikely that your site will be so large that it will require this feature, but if the designer has had experience in it, it's another talent in the bag of tricks he or she will bring to the job.

What Other Websites Has the Designer Been Responsible For?

Ask for the URLs of other sites the designer has created. And make sure at least one or two of them have been for small businesses that operate in a manner similar to yours (we'll look at how to evaluate a Website in a second).

Ask for References

Hiring a Website designer is no different from hiring an attorney, an accountant, or any other professional. Ask for two or three references and take the time to talk to them.

EVALUATING WEBSITES

After you've gotten answers to the preceding questions, you'll need to examine each candidate designer's work. The best way to approach this is to look at each site from the point of view of a customer and evaluate the following characteristics of the site.

APPEARANCE

First impressions mean a lot. Be aware of your initial response to appearance of the home page. Is it attractive and well-designed? Is there good use of color and graphics? Does it get all the important information across without being visually overwhelming?

DOWNLOAD SPEED

Time how long it takes pages to download. If you perform your evaluations with a 14.4 kbps modem, it will give you a good idea of the speed with which customers with the slowest Web connections will be able to download your site. This gives you a sort of worst case scenario, since anyone with a more updated connection will download it that much faster.

How fast is fast enough? With a 14.4 kbps modem, the slowest modem out there, a home page should download in 10 to 20 seconds. A 56.6 kbps modem will download the same page in about 3 to 5 seconds. And don't forget to try the site at different times of the day. During mid-afternoon almost all sites will be slower to download than during the early morning or late at night. There's so much more traffic on the Web during peak usage hours that everything is slowed considerably.

Pay attention, too, to how the home page downloads. Information will appear on your screen in bits and pieces when you download a page. The most important information, such as the name of the company, should appear quickly, with less important information and graphics taking longer to appear.

FILE SIZE

Here's a simple fact of life regarding Websites: the more files that are used to create a page, and the bigger those files, the longer it will take the page to download. You can monitor the size of the files on a home page by watching the status bar at the bottom of your Web browser. As each file begins to download, you'll see its size described in the status bar along with the speed with which it's downloading and the time remaining until the process is completed.

To measure download time, you can use this basic rule of thumb. Using a 14.4 kbps modem, one kilobit of data will take about a second to download. So a page with 20 kilobits of data will take 20 seconds to download. From there the math needed to figure download times with faster connections is simple. If you're using a 28.8 modem, the time is cut in half to 10 seconds. A 56.6 modem, 5 seconds. A cable modem will download it in the blink of an eye.

Obviously, the faster the Internet connection, the faster a page will appear on your monitor. But even at faster speeds, files of 30 to 40 kilobits or more can be annoyingly time consuming to download. If you find that a designer is fond of using large files, it's a good sign that he or she may be more interested in creating mind-boggling visuals than in efficiently providing information.

EASE OF NAVIGATION

Is it easy to get from one place to another on the Website? Ease of use is critical if your site is to be successful.

One of the best ways to evaluate a Website's navigability is to compare moving around the site to moving around a store in the physical world. For example, no matter where you are in a real store, you always want to be able to leave if you want to. Likewise, you should always be able to get back to the home page from wherever you are in a Website. In a real store, you should always be able to get to the checkout counter quickly when you've finished shopping. You also want to get help quickly when you have questions. Both these options should be available to online shoppers, too.

The ultimate no-no in Website navigation is to have a visitor hit a dead end, where the only option is to literally back out by hitting the "back" button and returning to the previous page. If you find any dead ends on the sites you evaluate, it's a good reason to eliminate the designer from your list of candidates.

SELECTING MERCHANDISE

Does the site have a shopping cart feature? If not, how do customers select the merchandise they want to purchase? Is the process cumbersome and filled with a lot of annoying steps, or is it a matter of simply making a few clicks with your mouse?

PAYING FOR MERCHANDISE

Is it easy to get to the "checkout" page? Does the site accept credit cards? If so, is the information sent to a secure server? What other kinds of security features are offered? Is there a fax number and an address so customers who are leery of using their credit cards on the Web can still order merchandise? The last thing you want is to create difficulty for people who are trying to give you money.

GETTING INFORMATION

How easy is it to get product information or to get answers to other questions you may have? Is there an FAQ (frequently asked questions) option where you can go in search of information? Perhaps most importantly, is there an e-mail option so you can write directly to the company? This feature, and the prominent display of toll-free telephone numbers, fax numbers, addresses, and other important information, are critical in allowing customers to communicate with a company.

FINDING WEB DESIGNERS

Finding candidates to design your Website won't be a difficult task. The profession has exploded right along with the Web itself. Many Web designers advertise in the yellow pages, newspapers, and industry magazines. Most ISPs will be able to refer you to several Web designers. You can also do a search on the Web itself.

The most savvy designers do their own advertising right on the Websites they've created. They'll include a credit on the site's home page in the form of a link to their e-mail address. It's an easy way for interested clients to contact them. All you have to do is click on the credit and fire off a message.

For my money, however, the best approach is the same one I'd recommend for finding experienced professionals in other fields—word of mouth. If you know other business people who have Websites, ask them who their designer was and if they were happy with the person's work. Another good strategy is to find other business Websites you like and contact them to find out the name of the designer.

Although there certainly are advantages to working with a designer who lives in close proximity to you, it's not absolutely essential. One of the wonders of the Web is the ability it gives people who are on opposite sides of the globe to work collaboratively on all kinds of projects, including Websites. It's entirely possible for you to find candidates, interview them, review their work, work out a contract with the one you decide to use, and get your site designed without the two of you ever actually meeting face-to-face.

How Much Will You Pay?

This is extremely difficult to predict. Website design prices are all over the board. Some designers charge by the hour. Others charge by the page. Some charge a flat rate based on the size of the site.

Most small businesses can count on spending from $1,000 to $10,000 to develop their Website. The variables influencing the final price include the size of the site, the number of graphics, whether you need to have a writer involved, whether you include interactive elements like surveys or other customer feedback, and your need for other features such as a shopping cart and audio/video options.

DESIGNING YOUR WEBSITE

Once you've selected a designer, the two of you will begin the design process. I say "the two of you" because this will very much be a collaborative process. Your job is to explain as accurately as possible the nature of your business and your goals for the site. The designer's job is to interpret your needs and let them drive the design of the site. It sounds simple, but in reality it can be very time consuming and laborious.

Above all else, a Website must be easy to use. If your customers can't find what they want quickly and easily, they'll leave and never come back. Here are the critical elements of a well-designed Website:

GOOD ORGANIZATION

Creating a useful Website begins with good organization. This, in turn, requires careful planning. This will be the first task you and your designer take on. It will probably also be the most annoying and the source of the most friction between the two of you.

The difficulty will largely be determined by the size of the site. How many pages will you need for your business? In what order will they appear? How will they be linked to other pages? These are just a few of the questions you'll need to consider.

This is why you need to hire someone with experience. I mentioned earlier that, among all their other talents, good Web designers are part tour guide. This is because they have the ability to create a map of your site that will serve as the basis for the final design. It's kind of like pulling together all the pieces of a puzzle, only you have to create the pieces as well as assemble them.

EASE OF NAVIGATION

This is the result of a carefully planned and designed site. It begins with a well-designed home page that gives visitors the overview of the larger site. From there they should be able to do two important things. One, they'll see where to go next to accomplish whatever it is they want to accomplish. And two, they'll be able to easily figure out how to get there. The best Websites are logical and intuitive. They're designed in such a manner that visitors can navigate through them with a minimum of effort.

Ease of Identification

When a customer visits your Website, two things should be immediately apparent—your business name and your product or service. All other information is secondary.

Pertinent Content

Web designers have all sorts of fancy tricks at their disposal, and a quick tour of the Web is evidence that many of them have had a hard time showing restraint. My pet peeves are copy that blinks on and off, animated graphics, and other bells and whistles that serve no apparent purpose other than to massage the ego of the designer. Many sites are like online versions of the Las Vegas strip. All the glitz may be impressive for a few seconds, but all it really does is distract visitors from what they're looking for.

It's important to keep the content of your site direct and to the point. You would never have a twenty-foot-high blinking neon sign outside your business in the physical world, right? There's certainly no reason to have one in cyberspace, either.

Quick Download Time

This is another reason to keep it simple. All those graphics and other fancy tricks take forever to download. If your customers have to sit there for thirty seconds every time they click on a new page, they're going to quickly lose interest in whatever it is you're selling.

Proper Window Size

Big Web pages are impressive, but only to those who have big monitors on which to view them. Keep in mind that most computer users operate with twelve- to fourteen-inch screens. This means you should stick to the standard window size of 640 pixels wide by 480 pixels high. Anything larger will require visitors to scroll up and down and from side to side to see everything on your pages. If you've ever had to do this, I don't have to tell you how annoying it is.

CLEARLY WRITTEN COPY

I know a number of editors who have spent their careers carefully tending the written word. They are without exception appalled at the poor grammar, improper punctuation, misspelling, and other mistakes all too often found on Websites.

Remember, you may be operating in a new environment, but that doesn't mean that the rules of written communication are out the window. In fact, if anything, they're more important than ever. For the moment, the written word is still the main form of communication on the Web. To treat it with any less care than you would anywhere else will only make you look like an idiot and diminish your credibility.

Does this mean you should hire a writer to help you write the copy for your Website? Yes, by all means, particularly if you have an extensive site. The copy should be short, crisp, to the point, and unambiguous. If you prefer to produce your own copy, at least hire an editor to take a look at your efforts, both before and after it's been put on your site. Mistakes do happen in translation, after all.

INTERACTIVITY

This is just Web jargon for the ability of merchant and customer to communicate with one another. It's a must if you're going to create a user-friendly site. Studies of Web use have found that interactive sites are more popular than those that aren't interactive. They get more traffic, and that means more business.

Interactivity is critical to selling online because it gives customers the ability to ask questions and get information, and that generates confidence and trust. Without it, shopping in cyberspace would be like sticking your money through a slot in a brick wall. If you ordered something from an online merchant with whom you couldn't communicate, and the merchandise either never arrived or there was a problem with it, you'd have just one option, sending it back. And you could only accomplish that if there was a return address.

Interactivity is equally important to merchants. In the physical world, you rely on your customers to give you feedback on your product or service. It's critical in meeting their needs and desires. The same thing is true in cyberspace. If you can't communicate with your customers, you'll never be able to fine-tune your business in response to their demands. Remember, business is anything but static. If you can't change with your market, you'll quickly be in trouble.

There are any number of ways to create an interactive site. The simplest is to have an e-mail link that customers can use to contact you. You can also include a "guest book" in which people can leave their names and e-mail addresses, a survey form that allows them to give you feedback on your site and your merchandise, a mailing list like Jim Spitznagel's that you can use to send out new product information, and even a discussion group where your customers can communicate with one another.

SEARCH TOOLS

Search tools are necessary features for larger sites in which standard navigation tools may not be sufficient to allow visitors to easily find their way around. They can range from a simple map of your site to an index to a special keyword search tool.

THE BASIC ELEMENTS OF YOUR WEBSITE

All business Websites, regardless of size, have a number of common elements. Depending on your goals, there are additional features you can add to make your site more useful to your customers.

HOME PAGE

This is the first page most customers will see when they arrive at your site. As I mentioned earlier, it's the equivalent of your storefront. It will include the name of your business, your logo (if you have one), and a table of contents that will take customers to underlying pages.

For example, if you visit Jim Spitznagel's Ithaca Music Shop (*http://www.jims.com/*), you'll see that Jim's home page has the name of his business along with his street address, phone and fax numbers, and his e-mail address. He also has links to a number of secondary pages. One link, "The Scoop on Jim's," provides visitors with basic information on the business. Another, "Dexter Sez," has up-to-date news about the business. Two others, "The Hip List" and "The $8.00 List," take customers to Jim's inventory. There's also a link to an order form and another to a page where customers can subscribe to Jim's new release list. Once they've signed up, they'll receive regular notices about new CDs that Jim has added to his inventory. From wherever you are in the site, you can always click on the icon that says "Back to the Main Pad," which will return you to the home page.

You'll also notice that these links are presented twice on Jim's home page. They're spread across the page in a graphic form in the person of Dexter, the cartoon beatnick that Jim has used as his alter ego and mascot since his days as a shopkeeper in Pittsburgh. But they also appear in text form at the bottom of the page. This is a common feature on Websites. It allows people who choose to view Websites without downloading graphics to navigate from page to page. (You can accomplish this with the controls in your browser. Ignoring graphics allows pages to download much quicker.)

When it comes to the design of your home page, remember that famous dictum of the architect Mies van der Rohe: "Less is more." It's quite appropriate, because you also are an architect of sorts—one who's concerned with the efficient spatial use of the seventy or so square inches of computer screen your customers will be sitting in front of. The last thing they need is to be bombarded with tons of copy and endless graphics. That just makes it difficult for them to find their way around. Keep it simple.

TABLE OF CONTENTS

All Websites need a table of contents. This tells visitors what can be found at the site and, with a click of the mouse, allows them to go to whatever interests them. Some home pages include a table of contents in the form of a "navigation bar," a highlighted box with all the navigation options included in text. Others, like Jim's, may use small graphic representations and text.

Hyperlinks

Your table of contents or navigation bar will appear on your home page as a series of "hyperlinks." The ability to create hyperlinks, or "links," is one of the features of Web technology that make the Web such a remarkable tool. Hyperlinks are created with hypertext, a simple form of HTML coding. They allow Web users to instantly move from one place to another in your Website with the click of a mouse. They can also go to any other sites you may have linked from your site. As I mentioned in Chapter 3, links are denoted by underlined text or graphics.

Every page in your Website should have links back to your home page and to your order form or "checkout" page. Depending on the size of your site, all your secondary pages may also be linked to one another. Your designer will help you determine what other links to create based on your needs.

One important point, though. Too many links on a page can confuse the customer. Encountering two links is like coming to a fork in the road. You can choose to go this way or choose to go that way. Three links are like an intersection. Four links are an even bigger intersection. More than six or seven and you can really begin to cause indecision in your visitors.

Another important point: keep your links arranged orderly in one spot on the page, such as in a navigation bar down one side or across the bottom. If they're scattered haphazardly all over the place, they'll be that much more difficult to use.

Secondary Pages

These are the pages visitors travel to from your home page. They will include the pages listed in your table of contents. Each one should represent a major subset of your overall site. Jim's Ithaca

Music Shop, for instance, has six secondary pages, each of which contains pertinent information his customers will need to know. Two of the secondary pages, "The Hip List" and "The $8.00 List," are jumping-off points for his inventory. From each one shoppers can roam deeper into the site to look through Jim's alphabetically arranged offerings. When they're ready to pay for their selections, they can go to another secondary page, the order form.

Think of secondary pages as the different departments in your electronic store. Let's say you have an online golf business that offers seven categories of merchandise—woods, irons, putters, balls, bags, shoes, and apparel. Each of these categories would have a secondary page that's listed in the table of contents on your home page.

Once customers go to a secondary page, there may be links to other pages that divide the merchandise up even further. For example, when your golf shop customers click on the link for the "irons" page, they may find that the page contains links to different manufacturers. One link might take them to the various Callaway irons you carry. Another to those manufactured by Cobra. Another to Titleists. Depending on the size of your inventory, you may have all your other categories divided up in a similar manner.

What's New

This is another link that should be found on your home page. Think of it as the equivalent of the sign down at your favorite butcher shop that says, "This Week's Specials." It's a place to announce special promotions or important news about your product or service. The term "What's New" for this kind of information has been popularized by online companies such as Yahoo, but you can call it whatever you wish. Jim calls his "Dexter Sez." It still gets the message across.

Product or Service Information

This information will be included on a secondary page (if you can make it brief, you can include it on your home page). It should give the customer complete information about your products and/or services and serve as an enticement to get them to move further into your site to learn more.

COMPANY INFORMATION

This is the nuts and bolts stuff about your business. It will include your company name and address, phone numbers, fax numbers, and e-mail address. If you wish, you can also include a bit about the history of your business, your goals as a business person, and other information. And remember to include a contact person your customers can ask for to get information. It can be you or a designated customer service representative.

FEEDBACK

This gets back to the interactivity issue. Your ability to monitor your customers' reactions to your business and your Website is critical to your success. If people don't like what you're selling or find your site difficult to use, you need to know, and quickly.

Obviously, you can accomplish this with e-mail. It's certainly the cheapest route. The downside is you have to go through your messages and weed out the ones from customers from those that pertain to other aspects of your business.

A more efficient method is to set up a separate link designated solely for customer feedback. It works well from a customer service aspect, too. The fact that you have a page devoted to their comments helps build your credibility and earns their trust. That, in turn, makes them more willing to patronize your business.

OTHER IMPORTANT DESIGN CONSIDERATIONS

Hopefully, by now you've spent enough time on the Web to realize there are a lot of sites that, regardless of whether they're easy to use, are just awful to look at. Here are some of the design concerns you'll need to keep in mind when creating your site:

TEXT AND BACKGROUND COLOR

Here's a guaranteed way to send your customers fleeing in droves from your Website. Use magenta text on a bright blue background. Or red on black. Or almost any color-on-color arrangement. If the text is small, it will make the problem even worse.

If your customers can't read your information, they're not very likely to do business with you. So stick to basics. Use black text on a white background for the bulk of your copy. Save the color for headlines and small blocks of copy to which you want to call attention. Keep in mind, too, that many people will print out pages from the Web to read later on. If you have colored text against a dark background, it will be even more difficult to read when it's printed. Likewise, if you use a light-colored text, such as yellow, against a white background, it will be equally difficult to read when printed.

TYPE SIZE AND STYLE

This one's simple. Make your copy in a large enough type size, or font, so it's easily read. Use larger font sizes for heads. Avoid small copy at all costs.

You can experiment with different fonts and different styles. Using a bold typeface will call attention to copy you want people to notice. You can also use italics for more emphasis.

Try different fonts to see which ones you prefer. Many designers feel the serif fonts, such as the one used in this book, are easier to read than sans serif fonts, which look like this. I've seen some in both styles that I find difficult to read. Let your eyes be the judge, and don't sacrifice legibility for style.

COPY LAYOUT

Despite all the advantages offered by the Web, few people enjoy reading large amounts of copy from their monitors. Many people, me included, will print out a long document and read it in hard copy rather than slog through it on the screen.

The lesson to be learned here is to keep your copy short and to the point. And don't run your copy from one side of the screen all the way to the other. That makes it extremely hard to read. Rather, use smaller and narrower blocks of copy or a single column with wide margins. Another good idea is to leave a space between paragraphs if you're presenting a lot of information.

The best idea is to use bulleted lists when at all possible. They present information in the most concise way possible and make it easier for customers to quickly learn about your business and your product or service.

IMAGES AND GRAPHICS

Images and graphics should enhance, not dominate, your Website. When considering an image, ask yourself a simple question: Does it serve a purpose? If it doesn't, don't use it. It just takes up space on your site and increases download time.

Once you decide to use an image or graphic, the critical issue becomes how large to make it on the page. A well-designed Web page should have a nice balance of copy and visual elements while still allowing a fair amount of "white space." If you want customers to have the option of viewing an image in a larger size, your designer can create a link from the smaller image to a larger image. This can be particularly useful if you're selling items that need to be seen in detail by your customers. If they're that interested in seeing it, they won't mind the extra time it takes for the image to download.

GIFs OR JPEGs

Another decision you'll need to make is whether to use GIFs (Graphics Interchange Format) or JPEGs (Joint Photographics Expert Group, a graphics format that compresses data) for your images. There are advantages and disadvantages to each. Because they're compressed, JPEG files are almost always smaller than GIF files. JPEGs also have a broader palette of colors, which will be important if you rely on images of your products to appeal to customers.

GIFs, on the other hand, are attractive because the background can be made to appear transparent, leaving the image silhouetted against the page. JPEGs always appear in a conventional square or rectangular format. GIFs can also appear in a series to create an animation effect.

Personally, I prefer JPEGs to GIFs. They're more crisp and their colors are more accurate. Your site designer will be able to fully explain the differences between the two and help you decide which is best for your site.

PAGE LENGTH

Unlike the physical world, where page length is determined by the size of a sheet of paper, pages on the Web can be many times "longer" than the dimensions of a monitor. The only problem is that reading them requires endless scrolling to get at all the material. Keep your pages at the dimensions I mentioned earlier—standard window size of 640 pixels wide by 480 pixels high.

One question many Web rookies ask is why they can't just scan their print advertising and use that on their Website. It makes sense. After all, they've probably paid an ad agency a hefty sum to create the ad, and they'd like to get as much mileage out of it as possible.

The problem is that a full-page 8½-by-11-inch ad won't fit on a computer screen. For one thing, the page is in a vertical format while the screen has a horizontal format. A second problem is that on a 640 by 480 pixel screen, only about a third of the page would be visible at any one time. Viewers would have to scroll vertically and horizontally to see everything on the page. Another problem is the size of the file that would be created. It would take forever to download, and even if it could all be seen at once, your customer would be long gone by the time the entire page was visible.

ADDING ALL THE BELLS AND WHISTLES

Most small business Websites use just text and graphics. But for those business owners who want to jazz up their sites and have extremely healthy budgets, there are a few additional options. Video, audio, animation, multimedia, and even virtual reality can be used to help you attract customers' attention and improve the display of your products.

Several words of warning, however. All these technological tricks carry with them an enormous potential for overkill. As I mentioned earlier, some sites end up looking like the Las Vegas strip or sounding like Times Square on New Year's Eve. Keep this in mind when working with your designer. Exercise restraint and practice good taste.

Also, in order to be seen and heard, most of these features require special applications and hardware that many Web users have no interest in obtaining. So you may be wasting time and effort (not to mention money) if your customers aren't up to speed enough to witness all the great stuff you've put together for them.

Here, in brief, is information on these options:

ANIMATION

The most common form of animation on the Web is achieved with a series of GIFs that are displayed in rapid succession, much like a slide show. The problem is, the more images you use, the bigger the file you create. So once again you're forced to make a decision between achieving a certain amount of "Wow" factor and keeping your site user-friendly. If you start to become overly tempted by the technology, keep in mind that user friendliness should always be priority one.

A more recent development in Web animation are vector-based graphics. These require much less file size than GIFs and allow visitors to stop and start the animation. There are also a number of animation software programs on the market that your designer may be familiar with.

The simplest form of animation on the Web is an HTML code that makes text "blink" on and off like a neon sign. For this reason, it's the most overused feature on the Web. Avoid it at all costs. To seasoned Web users it screams "bad taste!"

AUDIO

Audio can greatly enhance a site when used correctly. You can never go wrong with pleasant background music, and some people prefer the sound of a human voice to reading text. The only visitors to your site who might object to audio are those who are logging on from the office when they're supposed to be working. There's nothing like a sudden burst of music or voices to tip off your colleagues to the fact that you're surfing the Web instead of getting ready for that big afternoon meeting.

Some audio files on the Web are conventional recordings of music, voices, or sound effects. Others are synthesized sound that are in a format known as MIDI (Musical Instrument Digital Interface). They can be set up to play automatically when your site is opened or they can be selected by your visitors. There are several different file formats used on the Web, and your designer can help you determine which ones you need.

As with animation, the down side to audio is the size of the files it requires. And, predictably, the better the quality of the sound, the greater the size of the file. One solution to this problem is "streaming audio," which, because it's played as it's delivered to your customer's computer rather than waiting until it's downloaded, requires little waiting time and has excellent sound quality. Of course, you'll pay dearly for the benefits in the form of licensing fees for the proprietary software that's required. You'll also need a server that can handle the enormous amount of transmission line capacity, or bandwidth, that streaming audio needs. It's really an expense few small businesses can rationalize, even if they can afford it.

VIDEO

Video is another fun but prohibitively expensive addition to your site. There are currently two main technologies for delivering video over the Web. The first is a video file that's downloaded and played back by your customers. The second is streaming video, which, like streaming audio, can be seen as it's "fed" to your customers' computers rather than after it has finished downloading.

Frankly, video has a long way to go before it's a viable medium on the Web. In my opinion, it's not worth the cost and the trouble. The image quality of conventional video files is still quite primitive when compared to television, and the files themselves are enormous and take forever to download. Streaming video, while easier on the user, has even greater problems with image quality. And like streaming audio, it requires expensive licensing arrangements with the holders of the necessary software and an enormous amount of bandwidth. It also places software requirements on your customers, who may not be inclined to go to the trouble.

MULTIMEDIA

Multimedia is exactly that—a combination of video, audio, and interactivity that allows your customers unprecedented access to you and your products. Let's say you're selling furniture on the Web and you have a customer who's interested in a certain chair. Multimedia would allow her to rotate the chair to get different views while listening to an audio track that describes the item's features. If she wished, she could download images of the chair to her own computer for later viewing.

Like all these other technologies, multimedia has the same annoying problem of huge file size and lengthy download time. It's also still largely in the developmental stage. But eventually it will become more common and useful.

VIRTUAL REALITY

It's still a long way off, but there's little doubt that virtual reality will make its way to the forefront of Web technologies. When it does, imagine that every time a customer enters your Website they're greeted by . . . YOU! It's not that farfetched to think you'll be able to have a small, animated image of yourself accompanying visitors through your site. Rather than clicking on text or icons, they'll follow you from one page to another in your cyberbusiness. When that happens, online businesses will be more like real businesses than ever before.

One note about all of this. Along with many other aspects of Web technology, all these options will no doubt be made more efficient, and less expensive, in the next few years. Keep them in the back of your mind and pay attention to new developments. If they do get to the point where they're feasible additions to your Website, you should be ready to incorporate them.

WHAT'S NEXT?

Once you have your Website designed, it will be time to get ready to do business. You'll also have some public relations to take care of. One of the big hurdles to the growth of online commerce has been the reluctance of consumers to send their credit card numbers out over the Web. Some avoid the problem by printing out order forms and sending them via the U.S. Postal Service. Others fax them in. But a significant number simply refuse to consider shopping online.

With so much money at stake, this issue has received an enormous amount of attention, and the problem—if there ever was one—has been eliminated. Still, there's a lot of education to be done. Until all customers are comfortable with this new way of shopping, your online business could be missing out on a lot of sales. We'll look at the issue of online transactions in Chapter 7.

FOR MORE INFORMATION

Here are a few Websites that may be of help to you in building your Website.

➡ **Web Site Garage** (*http://www.websitegarage.com*) This Web-based service station is operated by professional Web designers who will critique your site and give you feedback on what works and what doesn't. You merely type in your URL and the garage will give you a five-point report that analyzes load time, looks for links that don't work, checks for spelling errors, and gives an overall critique of your site. It also counts how many other sites are linked to yours. You can use their report to make adjustments to your site or, if you wish, hire the garage folks to do it for you.

➡ **Web Developer.com** (*http://www.webdeveloper.com*) This is an online repository for articles, columns, and tutorials from Web Developer magazine. It also features an electronic forum where you can post questions and get advice from experts.

➡ **Webmonkey** (*http://www.webmonkey.com*) This site is operated by the people who publish *Wired* magazine and offers style tips for writing on the Web.

➡ **Alexa** (*http://www.alexa.com*) Alexa allows you to download a program that, when run while looking at a site, tells you who registered the domain name and the number of pages the site contains. It also rates the site's speed and its popularity. The really fascinating part of Alexa is its archive feature. The company maintains a complete historical record of the Web, and Websites that are no longer up on the Web can still be found in Alexa's archives.

7

CHECKS, CYBERCASH, CREDIT CARDS & SECURITY: CONDUCTING YOUR ONLINE TRANSACTIONS

Consumers purchased more than $2 billion worth of merchandise over the Web in 1997. By 2000 that number should pass $10 billion. And over the first decade of the new millennium, as more and more people come online and the paranoia that currently prevents some people from shopping in cyberspace is eliminated, the Web as a medium for selling will go right through the roof. I don't think there's any question that online sales will eventually equal or even surpass those generated by traditional mail order businesses.

That's a lot of money changing hands. So it's not surprising that the issue of how to exchange money in cyberspace ranks right up there with having a well-designed Website in the minds of cyberentrepreneurs. This chapter looks at the various methods you can use to conduct your online transactions. They range from the affordable to the extremely expensive. As you've probably figured by now, like most other aspects of setting up your site, you're limited only by the depth of your wallet.

How a company chooses to make financial transactions with its customers depends on the size and nature of its business. Small companies like Jim Spitznagel's compact disc business are usually able to function just fine using e-mail transactions. Big companies like L.L. Bean, on the other hand, need specially designed—and enormously expensive—programs that are tied directly into their inventory and shipping departments.

We'll also look at the security issue. The fears that some people have about shopping on the Web aren't entirely unfounded. But they certainly are exaggerated. There are also concerns that you as an online merchant must be aware of. We'll look at those as well.

DOING IT THE OLD-FASHIONED WAY

Some Web merchants choose to use their sites as the equivalent of a printed catalog. Their customers can view the merchandise, but when it comes time to place an order, they have to do it over the phone, with a fax, or by snail mail.

For a small Web business—particularly one that complements an existing storefront business—there's really nothing wrong with this approach. It depends on what you're selling as much as anything else. To make a purchase, your customers simply pick up the phone and call.

FAXING AND MAILING ORDERS

The "pick up the phone and call" approach may work fine for some companies. But for most businesses, I think this kind of arrangement makes the process a bit too inconvenient for the customer.

You really need to give your customers a variety of options for payment. Hopefully, most will be comfortable paying with a credit card, so a secure credit card transaction system is a must. (We'll look at the issue of security later in the chapter.)

Unfortunately, however, you will have a number of customers who aren't comfortable sending their card information over the Web. You need to have several options for them. A toll-free telephone number will allow them to phone their orders in. They should also be able to print out your order form and either fax it in or send it through the mail.

SET UP ACCOUNTS FOR YOUR CUSTOMERS

If you have repeat customers, and they prefer to do business this way, have them set up an account and let them charge their purchases. This is one way you can keep them happy and save yourself the fees banks will charge you for credit card transactions.

It's quite easy, and also secure. First, all customers who open an account with you are assigned a password they must use to validate their purchases. You'll have each customer's address on file and—this is the key to security—you'll have a policy that you'll only ship orders to that address. This arrangement makes stealing a customer's password pointless. Even if a crook was able to get a password and attempt to order merchandise with it, the order would still be shipped to the customer's address. The only way he's going to get it is to sit on their front porch and mug the delivery guy when he shows up.

Billing, too, is easy. You just send your customers their bills each month via e-mail. No postage, no paper, no envelopes. Then your customers simply mail you a check.

There are some disadvantages to this system. First, it will require you to do a credit check on every customer who opens an account, which can be quite annoying and time consuming. You'll also have to establish payment policies. How often will you bill your customers? After every purchase? Each week? Once a month?

Will you require full payment? More than likely. You're a retail business, not a lending institution, and cash flow will be critical. Finally, what happens if people don't pay their bills? You'll have enough to do already. Tracking down deadbeats just takes more time away from your business.

Nevertheless, this system will work, if you carefully select those to whom you extend credit. It might even serve as an enticement for them to spend more than they normally would.

ELECTRONIC PAYMENT SYSTEMS

There are several electronic payment systems you can use to attract customers who aren't comfortable using their credit cards for Web transactions. To use these systems, you need to establish an account with the vendors, who will supply you with the proper software. Customers also must have accounts in order to use the systems.

Costs for these payment systems vary. Depending on the vendor, you may be charged a flat fee when you receive the software; you may have to pay a monthly service fee; or, as with credit card purchases, you may have to pay a percentage of each transaction.

Here are some of the companies that offer electronic transaction systems.

DigiCash (http://www.digicash.com)

Digital cash is an inevitable development for doing business in cyberspace. It's an alternative to using credit cards, and because it's a secure system, it hopefully will let paranoid card owners become happy Web shoppers.

DigiCash uses an electronic currency called "e-cash" that customers can use to purchase goods and services over the Web. Customers obtain e-cash from participating banks, which debit the customer's real cash account. The e-cash is then stored as a credit on the customer's computer. When the customer makes a purchase, he transfers the appropriate e-cash credits to the merchant as payment. The merchant can then transfer the e-cash credits to his bank, which deposits the equivalent amount of real cash into his account. Customers are assigned a digital signature that lets them authenticate their transactions.

The obvious drawback to this system is that it only works if the customer, the merchant, and their banks all participate in the program. Unfortunately, that's not always the case.

CyberCash (http://www.cybercash.com)

CyberCash uses what's called an "electronic wallet" that users can download from its Website. The person enters his credit card number into the wallet, where it is encrypted. Then, rather than sending out his real card number when he makes a purchase, he uses the encrypted version of the number that's stored in the wallet. When the encrypted information is received by the merchant's software, it's sent to an authorization agency, where the transaction is either authorized or denied. The advantage of CyberCash is that neither the merchant nor CyberCash ever see the customer's real credit card number.

VERIFONE (*http://verifone.com*)

VeriFone also uses the electronic wallet system. Users can keep their credit card, debit card, or electronic cash information in the wallet. When they make a purchase from a business that uses VeriFone's system, they just transfer payment information to the merchant. It's a nice approach, but like most of these systems, it only works if both customer and merchant are users of VeriFone's software.

FIRST VIRTUAL (*http://www.fv.com*)

First Virtual's system is quite simple. Customers open an account with the company using their credit cards. They are then assigned a personal identification number that they use when making purchases. Merchants then contact First Virtual for purchase authorizations, and the purchases are charged to the credit card number that First Virtual keeps on file. The virtue of this system is that your credit card number isn't sent over the Web once it's in First Virtual's data base.

GCTECH (*http://www.gctech.com*)

This company has developed an effective but rather cumbersome system for paying for Web purchases. When a customer decides to make a purchase, he receives an electronic "payment request ticket." He sends the ticket back to GCTech with the information needed to complete the transaction, including a confirmation code, authentication information, and instructions for payment. The company then processes the transaction and sends a proof of payment to the customer.

ACCEPTING PAYMENT WITH CREDIT CARDS

The simplest way for customers to purchase goods over the Web—and for merchants to receive payment—is to use credit cards. Many people are quite comfortable with the idea. But there are some customers who, for whatever reason—media hype, distrust of technology, or just plain ignorance—refuse to send their credit card numbers over the Web.

This gets us to one of the most misunderstood issues about the Web—the question of whether it's safe to use your credit card to make purchases. Before we go any further, we need to take a closer look at this problem.

Is the Web Really That Unsafe?

I recently had an experience that illustrates how hysterical people are about this issue.

I was having dinner with a friend who, although he's quite informed about technology and spends a lot of time online, shares the one irrational fear that keeps many people from shopping in cyberspace,

"I would never send my credit card number out over the Web," he said as he examined the bill the waitress had just left. "Who knows how many people would be able to steal it."

Then, with those words fresh out of his mouth, he pulled out his American Express card and handed it to our waitress, who disappeared through a set of doors to take care of the transaction.

"Stan," I said, shaking my head. "You worry about using your credit card on the Web, yet you just handed your card to a total stranger who's going to swipe the card through a reader and send your card number across the same wires that are used to send Web data. What's the difference?"

"The difference," he said with an annoying air of authority, "is that there aren't any hackers on the phone lines trying to intercept data. The Web is crawling with crooks who steal credit card numbers. Happens all the time. I've read about it."

Well, Stan was getting a little carried away. And his thinking reflects that of a sizable portion of people who use the Web.

They're absolutely scared to death of using their credit cards and sending other personal information over the Web.

This is not to say that the Internet and the Web are completely secure. Information that's sent over the Web, including credit card numbers, can be intercepted while it's en route to its destination. There are also hackers out there who just love spending their time trying to break into the computers of corporations, organizations, the government, and sometimes individuals, either for the sheer challenge of it or to conduct a little electronic pillaging.

It's the risk that's been overblown. Sure, you can have your number stolen in cyberspace. You also can have it stolen down at Manny's Dry Cleaners or at Easy Ed's Video Rentals. You can even have it stolen by someone rummaging through your trash looking for receipts or billing information. The point is, there's risk to everything we do, including using our credit cards. The chance of having your card number intercepted while making an online transaction is no greater than it is from using it to make purchases in the three-dimensional world.

AN IRRATIONAL PARANOIA

To tell you the truth, I've never been able to figure out where all this worry and misinformation came from. Perhaps we all watched too many cowboy movies in our formative years. Granted, the Web may be a frontier of sorts. But contrary to Stan's fears, and those of millions of others, it's not some no-man's-land where outlaws are lurking behind every cyber-boulder, waiting to relieve unwary passersby of their valuables. It just doesn't work that way.

Let's look at how information is transmitted over the Web. At any given second during the day or night, trillions of bits of data are flying around the world at practically the speed of light. Buried within those data streams—mixed in with the e-mail, the research information on Etruscan pottery, the sports scores, the biographies of the American presidents, and the X-rated pictures—are credit card transactions. The chance of someone being able to identify a sequence of data as a credit card number from within that endless torrent is so minuscule as to be laughable.

Secondly, the two most popular browsers currently in use on the Web, Netscape and Microsoft Explorer, use technology that encrypts transactions before they go out over the Web. These are extremely difficult to crack. In fact, the one time Netscape did have a security breach, it took the hackers who managed to break in nine days of high-speed computing time to do it. This hardly seems worth the trouble just to grab a few credit card numbers.

As far as I'm concerned, the chance of having your credit card number snagged by a hacker in cyberspace is less than it is through normal use in the physical world. If my friend Stan is really concerned about his number being stolen, he should watch out for dishonest salespeople, hope someone's not intercepting his conversation when he's ordering merchandise over his cell phone, or check to make sure he hasn't thrown out any intact receipts with his trash. Web crooks are the last thing he should be worried about. And even if his card number was somehow picked up off the Web and used for fraudulent purchases, the rules for liability are the same as in the physical world—he'd only have to cover a very small portion of the amount charged.

Getting Over the Fear

Still, the fact that my friend Stan is so paranoid about shopping in cyberspace is a concern to those who are banking on the growth of online commerce. He's an intelligent, educated person who functions rationally in most aspects of his life. His irrational fear, and that of millions of others who share his fear, means that there's a considerable portion of the population—people with money and healthy spending habits—who are avoiding this new marketplace. The Web won't reach its full potential as an environment in which to conduct business until their fears are allayed.

It's not just individuals either. When L.L. Bean first unveiled its Website in 1996, the company would not accept credit card orders over the Web. When online shoppers wanted to place an order, they had to follow the same procedures they would if they'd been sitting with the catalog in their lap. They could call L.L. Bean's toll-free number and use a credit card to make their purchase. Or they could print out the order form, fill it in, and either fax it to the company or mail it in.

The company has come around, of course, and now uses a security system developed by IBM that works in conjunction with features built into browser software. It really had no choice. Granted, the Web can serve as an electronic version of the company's catalog, but to make life easy for its customers (and to keep pace with its competitors) it had to start accepting orders electronically.

ENSURING SECURE TRANSACTIONS

Even though the dangers of shopping in cyberspace have been blown out of proportion, it's obvious that a significant number of consumers will never become comfortable with shopping on the Web unless strict security measures are in place. The threat of all that lost business has inspired the biggest players in the game—including some of the country's largest banks, credit card companies, computer companies, and software companies—to join forces to settle the issue. Here are some of the security strategies that are commonly used.

ENCRYPTION

When information is sent over the Internet, it's broken up into many smaller pieces to make it easier to send. Each piece then takes a circuitous, unpredictable route through many other computers before it reaches its destination, where it's reassembled by the recipient's computer. It's these brief, blink-of-an-eye passes through the other computers that create security problems. If someone wants to go to an awful lot of trouble, they can electronically (and illegally) monitor data as it passes by and try to fish out credit card numbers and other information.

This is why secure data transmission systems use encryption, which breaks data into a mass of garbled letters and numbers that can only be reassembled with the proper software. It's the most practical and safest way to protect information. It ensures that the data arriving at your computer is the same data that was sent, and that no one tampered with it along the way.

Encryption is not only used for data sent over the Internet, it can be used for important data stored in your computer. That way, if someone breaks into your computer, any information they steal will be gibberish without the proper decryption software.

Needless to say, encryption is, and will continue to be, big business. Browsers like Netscape and Microsoft Explorer routinely encrypt data they transmit. Netscape uses a protocol called Secure Sockets Layer (SSL) which is approved by the U.S. government. There are also many other software programs available that your ISP or Website designer can recommend.

CERTIFICATES OF AUTHENTICITY

Certificates of authenticity identify merchants in cyberspace and are a good way to earn the confidence of wary cybershoppers. For a fee, merchants can obtain an electronic certificate that verifies their identity and guarantees that their server is secure or uses encryption to protect data.

Certificates of authenticity can be obtained from VeriSign (*http://www.verisign.com*) and Thawte Consulting (*http://tha wte.com*). They review information given to them by applicants and conduct background checks before issuing a certificate. Once a merchant is certified, he is given an electronic certificate that's installed on his server computer and lets customers know that the transactions made on that computer are secured.

These firms also issue consumer identification numbers, which let online merchants know that customers are who they claim to be. Many Web watchers feel that eventually everyone who is involved in online commerce—whether buyer or seller— will be required to have some form of digital identification. This will be particularly important for online banking.

SET—THE ULTIMATE SOLUTION?

Hopefully, even the most paranoid shoppers out there will finally come around with the unveiling of the Secure Electronic Transaction Protocol (SET), an open, worldwide standard that should put the security issue out to pasture once and for all. Developed jointly by, among others, Visa, MasterCard, Microsoft, Netscape, GTE, and IBM, SET assures that everyone involved in a transaction—customer, merchant, and the bank issuing the card—have both privacy and security.

It works like this: Customers are issued what some are calling a "digital wallet" by their bank or other card-issuing institution. It's a piece of software they plug into either a Netscape or Internet Explorer browser on their computer. When they want to make a purchase, they input their credit card number and other information into the software. Merchants are also given SET-compatible software that receive and execute customer transactions. The banks use SET software to provide a link between the two parties and to close payment on a transaction.

To add further security, both customers and merchants are given individual digital signatures that both parties must enter to complete a transaction. That way, if the first line of defense—the software—should somehow fail, and a crook should attempt to use a fraudulent card number, his inability to enter the proper "signature" will prevent him from completing the transaction.

In essence, SET is an independent automated payment system that operates over the Web but uses its own software at every point in the process. All information is encrypted, which prevents anyone outside the payment process from being able to see customers' personal information.

As this book was being written, SET was undergoing pilot tests in Asian markets under the watchful eyes of Visa, Citibank, and IBM. Considering the economic clout of the companies backing the program, there's little question that SET will become the global standard once the bugs are ironed out.

PROTECTING YOURSELF

The issue of whether to use their credit cards on the Web is a decision all consumers ultimately have to make for themselves. There's little you as an individual business owner can do other than to promote the use of credit cards by keeping up-to-date with security issues and being prepared to answer questions about the issue. As a merchant in cyberspace, however, there are two security issues you need to be aware of.

CREDIT CARD FRAUD

The first issue is credit card fraud. Traditional mail order and other businesses in which credit card information is taken over the phone have always had higher incidences of credit card fraud than storefront businesses. Web businesses report that the problem is as bad if not worse than with mail order.

The challenge of authenticating a cardholder is more difficult in cyberspace than in any other business environment. Various strategies have evolved to get around this problem, all of which are cumbersome and not very customer-friendly.

To use a credit card to make a purchase, your customers will enter their card number and expiration date along with their name and address. It's extremely important that all the customer information is complete. Once you've received their information, you'll need to validate the cardholder's information and then pass the transaction and payment information to your processing company for payment authorization.

Encrypted Card Numbers

One way around the fraud problem is to only accept orders from customers who have encrypted card numbers and digital signatures to authenticate their identity. This virtually eliminates the possibility that the card is stolen. The downside is that it also limits the number of people that can do business with you. And even if all your customers did use some form of encryption software, there are many software options on the market, and it would be almost impossible for you to support them all. This is one reason so many people have such high hopes for the SET protocol.

Verify Addresses

As long as merchants have to accept unencrypted credit card numbers, they'll have to scramble to make sure their customers are who they claim to be. One of the simplest methods to avoid fraud is to verify customer addresses by comparing the address on the electronic order form with the address on record at the bank that issues the credit card. If a customer requests that the merchandise be sent to a different address, you're probably going to have to get on the phone and do some additional work to verify the customer's identity.

Over time, as you build a clientele, the credit card issue becomes less of a problem. You'll have records of repeat customers and that will allow you to process their orders without delay. New customers, however, will always need to be checked out.

Two-Stage Ordering

This is one of the most common methods of taking unencrypted credit card orders over the Internet. It's simple, but it does make your customers work a little harder than they might care to. To make a purchase, they send the order information over the Web. But they send their credit card information either by fax, phone, or in the mail. Once they've made an initial purchase and you have their information on file, they can make subsequent purchases by just sending you their name and address over the Web with their order. Businesses that operate in this manner often include a registration form that customers can print and then fill out for faxing or mailing, either to make a purchase or to change their credit card information.

BREAK-INS

The second thing you need to guard against is hackers who may try to break into your computers, either for sport or to steal information, including the credit card numbers of your customers.

One of the many tricks employed by cybercrooks is a program called a "keyboard sniffer." This program is surreptitiously inserted from the Internet into a business's computer or a nearby computer. Once there, it monitors all the information typed on the keyboard. When it spots an unencrypted credit card number, which is easy to recognize, the program sends the information out over the Web the next time the user goes online.

Your vulnerability to being hacked is determined by the number of computers your business has connected to the Internet. Without that direct link, hackers have no way to break in. Most small businesses are able to operate with just one or two, and security for a system this size is easy to control.

But for large businesses that have ten, twenty, or even more computers in a system, security can be an enormous problem. Each computer's Internet connection must be monitored, as well as connections between computers. Every possible link in the system is vulnerable, and if an intruder does somehow manage to tap into one of your computers, you need to make sure he can't get any further. This is the job of firewalls.

A firewall is a security checkpoint at a computer's entry and exit point for data, including Internet traffic. A good firewall lets you control what comes in and what goes out. For example, you can configure a firewall to allow only e-mail to pass back and forth. You can also make it a one-way street, where no traffic can come in from the Internet but you and your employees can access the Internet and Websites without restriction.

In lieu of firewalls, which are quite expensive, some businesses install routers and filter software that can identify and delete certain kinds of data that may pose a security threat. Some filter software can even filter traffic being sent out of your system.

Do You Need a Firewall?

For most small businesses, a firewall is an unnecessary expense, provided the computer they use to access the Internet and the Web is not used to store information they consider valuable or confidential (this is where the second computer I talked about earlier comes in handy). If you do keep information like the names and addresses of customers, credit card numbers, and personal business records on a computer that's connected to the Internet, however, a firewall is a must.

It's not that there are bad guys lurking outside just waiting to invade your computer. The chances of having a problem like this are really quite slim. But there's always the chance, and the damage they can do once they've gotten into your computer can be absolutely devastating to your business. In 1995, a legendary hacker named Kevin Mitnick stole 20,000 credit card numbers from an Internet access company called Netcom. In what would prove an embarrassing oversight, the company had them stored on an unsecured computer that was linked to the Internet. Based on Mitnick's history, it's un-likely he ever planned to use the numbers. Like so many hackers, who view computer security systems the way serious climbers view Mount Everest, he just did it to show that he could. Still, it's a good example of what can happen if you let your guard down.

BUYING A FIREWALL

You should consult with your Web page designer or hire a consultant to help you select a firewall. Also, find out if a router and filter would be equally effective. But once again, the best strategy is to avoid the need altogether by keeping all your valuable data on a stand-alone computer that's not connected to the Internet.

MINIMIZING YOUR VULNERABILITY

Protecting yourself from a break-in is simple. As I mentioned before, data can only be stolen from a computer that's con-nected to the Internet, either directly or through a network. It can't be stolen from a computer that's not connected to any-thing else.

So the answer is simple. You need two computers, one that's

connected to the Internet for taking orders, and the other for storing information. To protect yourself and your customers, you'll need to remove all the data about your customers from your Internet-connected computer as soon as possible after you receive an order. As long as the information sits there, it's vulnerable to hackers.

The easiest way to do this is to periodically transfer all your recent order information from your connected computer to a floppy disc. After running an antivirus program to make sure no bugs have arrived with the orders, you can then move the information to your stand-alone computer. And I do mean stand alone. The computer that you use for the permanent storage of information cannot be connected to anything, not even an e-mail program. Any link to the outside is a possible entry point for cybervandals.

ONE FINAL NOTE ON THE SECURITY ISSUE

None of the security systems discussed here are foolproof. In fact, it's unlikely that a security system will ever be developed that's 100 percent effective. That's because every time a new system hits the market, hackers like the aforementioned Mr. Mitnick will begin to pick away at it until they've figured out how to circumvent it. In response, the industry will unveil a new product, and that, too, will be dissected. This tit-for-tat game will probably never go away.

The lesson to be learned here is that to do business in this new environment, you need to keep pace with what's happening in critical areas like online security. There's a lot of money to be made in cyberspace, and entrepreneurs are hard at work to make it a safe place to shop. Part of your responsibility as a merchant is to monitor new developments in online security and make sure they're implemented on your site. It will keep your customers happy. And as all merchants know, happy customers mean more business.

WHAT'S NEXT

Doing business in cyberspace is often compared to doing business through mail order. There are a lot of parallels. But there's also one very big difference. In mail order you can easily contact your customers. It's a bit more difficult in cyberspace. There, more often than not you have to entice the customer to contact you. We'll look at how to call attention to your online storefront in Chapter 8.

FOR MORE INFORMATION

Here are a few excellent books that address in detail the issue of Web security and the safety of online transactions:

- ➡ *Web Security and Commerce* by Simson Garfinkel and Gene Spafford (O'Reilly and Associates, 1997)
- ➡ *Web Security Sourcebook* by Avi Rubin et al (John Wiley & Sons, New York, 1997)
- ➡ *Maximum Security: A Hacker's Guide to Protecting Your Internet Site and Network* by Anonymous (Sams, 1997)
- ➡ *Internet Security for Business*, Terry Bernstein, editor (John Wiley & Sons, New York, 1996)
- ➡ *Digital Cash: Commerce on the Net* by Peter Wayner (Ap Professional, 1997)
- ➡ *Electronic Payment Systems* by Donal O'Mahony et al (Artech House Computer Science Library, 1997)

8

"HELLO! HERE I AM!":
GETTING NOTICED ON THE WEB

The first time you punch your company's URL into your keyboard and see your Website appear on your monitor will be one of the most exciting moments in your business career. But here's a sobering thought that will bring you back to earth real quickly: there are fifty million Web users out there, and you're the only one who knows this thing exists!

In effect, you're at ground zero—lost and (temporarily) alone in cyberspace. This is where a Web business is different from almost any other kind of business. You have this great thing, this great place, this great business, and it's completely invisible. Nobody will ever find it unless you or somebody else tells them it's there. From this point on your primary job will be to get noticed by as many Web users as possible. This chapter looks at how it's done.

START WITH THE BASICS

Your first strategy in attracting people to your little corner of cyberspace begins in the physical world. You're operating in a new environment and you have a new address in that environment—your URL. Your first order of business is to get that address, and your e-mail address, in front of as many people as possible.

STATIONERY AND BUSINESS CARDS

We'll start with what seems obvious. But because it's so obvious, it's easily overlooked—add your new addresses to your business materials. Your URL and e-mail address must be on every business card, every piece of stationery, and every other piece of printed material that you use in your dealings with your customers, your vendors, and anyone else you have contact with. And don't wait until the site is finished to make the changes. Take care of them beforehand. The day the site is launched is the day you should begin using your new materials. (By the way, if space or stylistic issues ever require shortening your URL, feel free to eliminate the http:// prefix. It's not even required by most browsers anymore.)

ADVERTISING

Your URL and e-mail address must also be incorporated into your advertising. If you use primarily print advertising, they should appear prominently in every ad. Likewise for direct mail pieces. If you use television, make sure they're included in the ad and can be easily read. If you use radio, they should be included right along with your address and phone number.

You can also organize an entire advertising campaign around the launch of your site. If you'll recall the timeline presented in Chapter 5, one of the steps I recommend is to begin a public relations and advertising campaign four to eight weeks before you launch your site.

If it's handled correctly, an ad campaign can build a great deal of anticipation. One of the most memorable campaigns I ever saw was for the movie *Ghostbusters* back in 1984. Several months before the movie was released, its studio placed little ads in some of the nation's leading newspapers. All they showed was the movie's ghost logo and a caption that said, "Coming this summer to save the world!"

Millions of people saw the ads, but nobody knew what they meant. Because they weren't always placed with the movie advertisements, the fact that it was a movie was cleverly disguised. This heightened the public's curiosity that much more.

By the time the big ad campaign hit around Memorial Day, those little ads had people primed to buy, see, or visit whatever the heck it was that was coming to save the world.

The lesson to be learned here is that ads that create a little mystery can also attract a lot of attention. This is actually what initially attracted me to Jim Spitznagel's site. He ran a small ad on the back page of the little community newspaper here in town that simply listed his URL—*http://www.jims.com/*. There was no clue as to what kind of business it was. When I discovered he sold compact discs, I was pleasantly surprised. But the fact that I didn't know what I'd find when I punched in his URL was the real attraction.

PROMOTIONAL ACTIVITIES

You're starting a new business. Just because it's on the Web doesn't mean you should treat it differently than if it were in a mall or downtown. You need to rely on the same promotional activities you would use for any business venture.

This is often overlooked by cybermerchants. For some reason, they think that an online venture should conduct all its promotional activities on the Web. As a result, they miss a lot of opportunities. Don't make the same mistake.

PRESS RELEASES

Businesses and organizations routinely announce important events by sending out press releases to newspapers, TV stations, radio stations, and other media. You can do the same for your Website.

A press release is not a sales tool. It's an announcement. It should be written like a news article and include the basic "who, what, when, where, and how" information that any news story uses. Make sure your URL, e-mail address, and phone number are listed.

Keep the release simple and to the point, with short declarative sentences and short paragraphs. Send it out on company letterhead and don't make it any longer than two pages. A week or so after you send it out, follow up with phone calls to your most influential recipients to make sure they got the release and to see if they need any additional information. That kind of personal contact also increases your chances of getting more media attention.

If you need to, hire a professional writer to help you draft your press release. It will be well worth the expense.

GRAND OPENING

"A grand opening in cyberspace?" you might ask. Sure. In fact, I think it's a great way to get attention. The day you launch your site, publicized by the methods we just discussed, you can have a grand opening at your physical location. Invite friends, clients, and the media. Serve refreshments. You might be surprised at the response you get, particularly from the media. Many reporters may have a working knowledge of the Web but don't know much about the technology behind it. The chance to get a "behind the scenes" look at how a Website really operates could really attract their attention. It could even result in a story.

RECIPROCAL LINKS

This is the "I'll scratch your back if you scratch mine" approach to getting attention. As you'll recall from Chapter 3, links are underlined words or icons that, when clicked, take a Web surfer to a new Website. When someone clicks on a link with your URL, no matter where they are on the Web, they'll be delivered right to your site. So the more links you have out there, the greater your ability to bring customers to your door. You can create links by contacting the operators of other Websites and asking them to create a link to your site. In return, you agree to create one to their site.

There is an important consideration in using this strategy, however. As you'll learn from my interview with Jim Spitznagel in Chapter 12, you need to be very careful about the kinds of businesses you link to. In a sense, they're a reflection of your own business. If they engage in poor business practices and have lousy customer service, do you really want to be associated with them? Jim avoids the issue altogether. He refuses to link with anyone.

SEARCH ENGINES AND DIRECTORIES

Your next step is to add your URL to the search engines and directories that people use to locate information on the Web. Some directories specialize in certain businesses or industries. Others have general information. Many will add your URL for free.

Search engines help make the Web an incredible tool for getting information on almost anything you can think of. They work by scanning the Web for sites whose URLs and site information match the keywords entered by a user. For a very simple example, let's say you wanted to find information on major league batting averages over the last fifty years. You might begin by typing the word "baseball" into the keyword box of a search engine. In a matter of seconds the engine would provide you with a list of Websites related to baseball. From there the best search engines will allow you to refine your search even further by entering "batting averages" into the keyword box. The search engine would then provide you with a list of sites that contain batting average information. The site lists generated by search engines are provided as links, allowing users to go right from the list to the desired site.

Submitting Your URL

If you choose to, you can submit your URL to a search engine yourself. You may need to write a description of your site that falls within guidelines set up by each directory. You'll also need to decide in which categories you want to be included, what keywords you want to associate with your site, and provide other information requested by the directory. Your description of your site should be brief and to the point, no more than twenty-five or thirty words. Some directories will reject your submission if the description is too lengthy.

Submitting your information may be tedious and time consuming, but it's not difficult. Most search engines have a button labeled something like "Add URL." Clicking on the button will open a registration form. You input your URL and any other information that's requested. In many cases all you have to do is enter your URL. The search engine takes care of the rest by dispatching a "Web spider" to your site to gather information.

If you find you have more important things to do with your time, you can hire a registration service to take care of getting your site submitted. Also, many ISPs will provide URL registration as part of a package of services to help you get your business up and running.

There are hundreds of directories out there, so you'll need to be selective in finding ones that pertain to your business. Regardless of which you choose, there are a few major directories that every business should register with. Here are my favorites. If you haven't used search engines or directories before, try them out to get a feel for how they work.

Excite (*http://www.excite.com*)
Yahoo! (*http://www.yahoo.com*)
Webcrawler (*http://www.webcrawler.com*)
Lycos (*http://www.lycos.com*)
Open Text (*http://www.opentext.com*)
Infoseek (*http://www.infoseek.com*)
HotBot (*http://www.hotbot.com*)
LinkStar Business Directory (*http://www.linkstar.com*)
Alta Vista (*http://www.altavista.com*)
Starting Point (*http://www.stpt.com*)
Mallpark (*http://www.mallpark.com*)
ComFind (*http://www.comfind.com*)
Companies Online (*http://www.companiesonline.com*)

The major directories get thousands of submissions every day, so it usually takes a few weeks before your site will appear. And make sure it does appear. It's easy for a submission to get overlooked. If it doesn't show up after a few weeks, send in

your information again. It might even take three times before
it shows up.

WEB SPIDERS

When you add your URL to a search engine's submission page,
the search engine sends a "spider" to your site to retrieve
information (some also use humans to take care of this chore).
Some spiders just do what's called a top-level search, meaning
they just examine your home page. Others do a second-level
search and follow all the links from your home page. Some
claim they go as deep into a site as possible and index every
page.

The best search engines update their information by revisiting
sites periodically to see what changes have been made. Companies that use spiders are able to accomplish this task faster than
those that rely on employees. Some of the major search engines
claim they can update their data bases in a week.

Even if you didn't register your site, chances are it would
end up in some of these directories anyway. That's because a
number of the above directories—including Open Text, Lycos,
Excite, Hotbot, Infoseek, and Alta Vista—use their spiders to
find new URLs. They act like electronic explorers, roaming the
farthest reaches of cyberspace at random looking for URLs they
don't recognize. When they find one, the send the URL and
other information back to the directory.

You may be tempted to leave all this to the fates and assume
that Web spiders will take care of the registration issue for you.
Don't do it. This is your business and your livelihood we're
talking about. It's not something to take chances with.

SPIDER SOFTWARE

If you want to streamline the registration process, you can buy
a spider software program that will automatically register your
site with hundreds of directories in just a few minutes. Most
cost in the $50 to $100 range, and upgrades are usually free.

Two of the most popular spider programs are SoftSpider
(*http://www.softspider.com*) and Web Promotion Spider (*http://*

www.beherenow.com/spider). Users of these programs, however, report mixed results. The programs make more than two
hundred submissions in less than an hour, but not all the submissions are always accepted, including those to some of the
major directories mentioned earlier. The programs do let users
know which ones weren't accepted. If you see one you think
is critical to your business, you can do a submission yourself.

REGISTRATION SERVICES

There are a number of businesses out there that will take care
of the registration process for you. Some will even do it for
free. One of the most popular is Submit It! (*http://www.submit-
it.com*), which offers both free and fee-based services. The free
service allows you to enter the information about your site, then
select from a menu of about twenty directories those to which
you want your information submitted. The fee-based service,
and others like it, offers submission to several hundred directories. Some services claim to have access to as many as five
hundred directories. Charges typically range from $50 to $100.

Is it worth it? Yes, if you end up in directories pertinent to
your business. But a lot of these companies are just firing blind,
sending out URLs to as many directories as possible with no
guarantee of results. Some may even be using the same spider
software you could buy yourself.

Because these firms offer no guarantees, the only way to find
out how successful the submissions were is to follow them up
yourself. If your URL doesn't show up in the directories to
which it was submitted, you can complain to the service business, which may or may not agree to submit it again. Or you
can do it yourself. My advice is to talk to a representative from
the service beforehand to find out what they will or will not do
to make sure the submissions are successful.

SPECIALIZED DIRECTORIES

As more and more businesses and organizations come online,
the need for specialty directories becomes greater and greater.
It just makes it easier to find what you're looking for.

After you register with the major search engines and directories, you'll need to find directories that specialize in your kind of business. There may be a fee involved, but if it's a good directory, it will be worth whatever it costs.

How Search Engines Work

When a search engine examines your site, it records various things about your business and enters the information into its data base. This data base is searched when a user makes a keyword request. The URLs of sites whose information matches the keyword are then given to the user.

Obviously, this means that the information the search engine records about your business is critical to whether your URL is given to users when they conduct a search. It also will have an effect on where your URL appears in the lists users are given. If a keyword search produces a list of two hundred sites, you'll want your site to be as close to the top of the list as possible (We'll look at how you can influence this later in the chapter.)

Here's what search engines remember:

Word Placement and Frequency of Use

Most search engines take note of how often a word is used in a site and where the word appears. For example, the words in the name or title of your URL will be heavily weighted. Words that appear close to the start of a page are also considered important. And the more those words appear elsewhere in your site, the more importance they'll be given.

Because word frequency can provide a Website a prominent place in the lists given to searchers, it didn't take site designers long to learn that "word-packing"—repeating a word over and over again—would throw off search results and move a site to the top of a list. Some search engines will automatically move a site deeper into a list if word-packing is suspected. Others don't bother checking for it.

Links

Some search engines note how many other sites have links to your site. The more links there are, the more popular your site is considered to be. And popularity is an important factor in determining where your URL will appear in lists given to search engine users.

Categories

Most search engines will place your site in a category with other sites in the same category. Some will allow you to select the category in which you will appear. Others will put you wherever they think you should go based on the information their spiders have gathered from your Website.

How Search Engines Rank Sites

After a search engine gathers information on your Website, it stores the data in a data base. When a user conducts a keyword search, the data base is scoured to find sites whose information includes those key words. A list of all the URLs that match is then given to the user.

Most search engine companies are fairly close-mouthed about how they rank sites. For one thing, they don't want their competitors to know what criteria they use. They also want to prevent Website designers from including information in a manner that will artificially move their sites to the top of a list.

Because of all the secrecy, the best way to figure out how search engines create their hierarchies is to spend some time with each one and do some searching of your own. Site designers and other people who spend a lot of time online are also good sources of information. Many have contributed their knowledge to a site called Search Engine Watch (*http://search enginewatch.com/*). Refer to this site for information on how you can influence your ranking.

ONLINE PROMOTIONS

This is an area that must be negotiated with great delicacy. In Chapter 3, if you'll recall, I briefly discussed "spamming." This is Internet lingo for the practice of sending out unwanted messages to thousands of computers at a time. Often, spammers will send their messages to newsgroups or mailing lists. They sometimes manage to infiltrate the e-mail systems of entire corporations or organizations so that every employee receives the message. It's the electronic equivalent of junk mail, and it's just about as popular with recipients. Some Internet experts estimate that as much as 10 percent of the e-mail traffic on the Web is spam.

If you have e-mail, you more than likely have been spammed. I've been hit with information about cruises and other vacation packages, golf-related come-ons, and a number of other ads. I rarely read them before I hit the delete button. (Well, okay. I'll admit I read the ones about golf. But I've never bought anything.)

BANDWIDTH ISSUES

The practice has raised the hackles of Internet denizens for a number of reasons. One is the amount of bandwidth that's wasted by such messages. As we learned earlier, the Internet and the Web are limited in the amount of data they can transmit at one time. The more data that's rushing around the world, the slower everything moves. If the 10 percent estimate is correct, that means there's a lot of junk mail out there holding up traffic.

Spamming is particularly problematic for ISPs and other sites that serve as Internet hubs. Traffic can get so backed up at these points that the movement of data slows to a trickle. In a worst case scenario, it can even cause service to halt altogether. For the ISP whose service is affected, this can lead to a lot of very unhappy customers.

If you were to suddenly send out a few thousand e-mail messages at once, you'd hear from your ISP real quickly. You'd be warned in no uncertain terms not to do it again. You might even find your service cut off if you caused enough of a disruption. Likewise, if you're an ISP that's being used as a conduit for incoming spam, you'll be equally angry.

ETHICAL ISSUES

To hide their tracks, many individuals and organizations that engage in spamming will put false information in the sender and reply address fields of their messages. This means the messages can only be traced back as far as the ISP that handled the spam on its way onto the Internet. And once again the poor ISP takes the heat.

LEGAL ISSUES

Should Internet users be allowed to live spam-free lives or do companies have the right to send out these unwanted mass mailings? Is it any different than sending out junk mail in the physical world? Are there issues of privacy involved? Are there issues of free speech? These are some of the questions being debated in the ongoing arguments over spamming.

Many of these questions may have been answered in March 1998, when Cyber Promotions, Inc., of Dresher, Pennsylvania, agreed to pay $2 million to settle the last of several lawsuits brought against it by Internet service providers, including America Online. Under the terms of the agreement, the company's president, Sanford Wallace (also known as the "King of Spam" and "Spamford" in some circles), will be personally liable for another $1 million if he or any company affiliated with him e-mails unsolicited advertisements to the subscribers of Earthlink Network, Inc., another of the firms that filed the suits. Earthlink, based in Pasadena, California, serves more than 450,000 customers. Cyber Promotions was considered the Internet's largest purveyor of unsolicited e-mail ads, sending as many as 25 million e-mail messages a day.

At about the same time the suit was settled, Washington became the first state in the nation to enact an antispamming law. The new law makes it illegal for spammers to use forged return addresses or to misrepresent a message's point of origin. California is investigating a similar measure.

So What Should You Do?

As I mentioned earlier, you need to tread lightly around this issue. Despite the problems, carrying out online promotions isn't completely out of the question. It just has to be handled judiciously. Some discussion groups and mailing lists will accept some commercial messages as long as they're relevant.

The best tactic is to be polite and up front by contacting the operators of discussion groups and mailing lists for permission to send information to the members. Explain what your business does and why you feel it may be of interest to the people on the lists. The worst thing that can happen is you'll be turned down. But if you make a reasonable case, chances are some operators will agree to let you post your message. If it brings some business your way, you'll have achieved a profit and avoided generating bad feelings.

You can also send out promotional messages to mailing lists you create on your own. If the people on the lists are legitimate customers, and the lists aren't outrageously long, you shouldn't have a problem.

Start Your Own Newsgroup or Discussion Group

There is one more approach you can take. Since you run the risk of attracting people's ire when you send out electronic ads to discussion groups and mailing lists, you can start your own, based on your product or service. For example, if your business sells golf equipment, you start a group devoted to golf.

You have two choices. One is to start a newsgroup on the Usenet. There are already about 40,000 newsgroups out there, with an estimated ten million readers, and more are being created all the time. They're different than discussion lists. They're like electronic bulletin boards that can be read by anyone on the Internet. Each one is devoted to a specific topic, and people post general questions or comments regarding that topic. Some people, called "lurkers," never participate but spend a lot of time monitoring what other people have written.

Discussion groups, on the other hand, are limited to people who subscribe to the list. Rather than appearing in a bulletin board format on the Usenet, discussion groups carry out their debates using e-mail. As I mentioned in Chapter 3, since messages go out to everyone in the group, they can generate a lot of traffic. The two times I belonged to discussion groups it wasn't unusual to have two or three dozen messages on my computer when I turned it on in the morning. When I would come back from a long weekend or a vacation, the backlog was unmanageable.

When you start a newsgroup or discussion group, you'll know that everyone who chooses to participate is interested in the product or service you provide. If you decide to follow this strategy, remember one important thing. You still can't send out advertisements or even press releases. That will anger a lot of people. Rather, the idea is to participate in the sharing of information and opinions with other members of the groups. You can do this as a representative of your business, using the business name. If you can answer questions and provide valuable information to other members of the groups, that in itself is extremely valuable publicity for your business. I'll guarantee you it will generate visits to your site and put money in your pocket.

You can also follow this strategy to post messages to existing newsgroups or discussion groups. Again, the key is to be a participant, not a promoter. People will still learn about you and your business.

ELECTRONIC NEWSLETTERS

An online newsletter is an excellent method to get information about your business to your customers. It can also attract new customers.

Newsletters are also a great way to build a mailing list. Rather than making the newsletter available at the push of a button, have a subscription form on your home page where people can submit their e-mail address if they want to receive it. As you get new subscribers, you can add their names to your e-mail list.

A good newsletter is not just an advertising tool. It provides updates on new products, tells people about your future plans for the business, and can even include input from customers and subscribers. It should be short—no more than two screens in length—and come out often enough that people expect to see it. (See my interview with Jim Spitznagel in Chapter 12 to see just how effective a newsletter can be.)

CREATE AN FAQ DOCUMENT

An FAQ (frequently asked questions) document is another way to provide information to your customers. You can create a link to an FAQ document from your home page. It should be written in question-and-answer format, with the most important questions listed first (a lot of people fail to read to the end of electronic documents). Update the document often to make sure it addresses new questions that may come up.

ONLINE ADVERTISING

One of the reasons for doing online promotions with e-mail is that it costs next to nothing. But since its effectiveness is minimal, and the potential for getting into trouble is enormous, you really need to look at online advertising.

Once commercial enterprises found their way onto the Web, it didn't take advertising long to catch up. You can now buy a rotating "banner" ad on a major search engine such as Yahoo! for around $1,000 a week. This means your ad shares the same space with the ads of other businesses. As viewers visit the page, the ads take turns appearing on the page. If there are ten ads sharing the space, every tenth visitor to the page sees your ad. The company guarantees 120,000 appearances of your ad each week.

Of course, since Yahoo! is one of the most popular sites on the Web, it can charge the highest prices. It's just like television or radio advertising. The bigger the market share, the more you'll pay.

But you might not need Yahoo! or the other big names, particularly if you're selling something that has a narrowly defined audience. If you find smaller sites you think might attract the kind of person who would buy your product or service, you can probably buy advertising space for much less.

WHAT'S NEXT

The above discussion of advertising is just the beginning of the subject. There's a certain psychology to advertising on the Web, and the techniques are becoming increasingly sophisticated. Marketing in cyberspace is also a very different animal. We'll look at both and why they're so important to your business in Chapter 9.

FOR MORE INFORMATION

The following books will give you additional ideas on how to attract attention on the Web.

➡ *Guerrilla Marketing Online: The Entrepreneur's Guide to Earning Profits on the Internet* by Jay Conrad Levinson and Charles Rubin (Houghton Mifflin Co., New York, 1997)
➡ *Cyberwriting: How to Promote Your Product or Service On-line (Without Being Flamed)* by Joe Vitale (AMACOM, 1996)
➡ *Marketing on the Internet: A Proven 12-Step Plan for Promoting, Selling, and Delivering Your Products and Services to Millions Over the Information Superhighway* by Michael Mathiesen and Jerry Yang (Maximum Press, 1996)

9

MAKING THE SALE: MARKETING AND ADVERTISING ON THE WEB

When you open for business, you'll be part of a market that has never existed before. It's one in which a customer on the other side of the world can purchase something from you with the same ease and speed as a customer who lives on the other side of town.

It's also a market in which your customers can learn everything they need to know about your business and its products or services by sitting in front of their computers and navigating through your site. There's no need to send for promotional materials, call an 800 number, or talk to a local service representative. E-mail, FAQ documents, and the information contained on your Website will provide them with everything they need.

So servicing your customers is easier and more efficient than ever with this new medium. But at the same time it makes advertising and marketing more difficult, or at least extremely confusing. It changes the way you reach your customers and also the messages you send them. But in the end, if you've done it correctly, you'll have achieved an intimacy with your customers that no other medium can come close to.

The bottom line is that the Internet and the Web require advertising and marketing with some new twists. This chapter looks at how they're different and what you'll need to do to conduct successful advertising and marketing campaigns.

WHY MARKETING AND ADVERTISING ARE DIFFERENT ON THE WEB

Marketing and advertising have traditionally been done through print media, broadcast media, direct mail, and telemarketing. While the Web has something in common with each of these, it's much more versatile. Marketing and advertising on the Web is a whole new ball game. What follows are some of the reasons why.

IT'S INTERACTIVE

This may be the biggest advantage the Web has over other methods of marketing. No other medium allows the kind of two-way communication between merchant and customer that the Web provides. Sure, a customer can make a phone call to a company in the physical world with a question about a product or to request that a sales brochure be sent in the mail. But the Web allows so much more.

A good example is Amazon.com's practice of greeting me by name when I log on and presenting me with a recommended list of books based on what I've purchased on previous visits. I can click on the book titles and be linked to the pages for each one so I can read about them. If I have a question, I can send the company an e-mail. As I make additional purchases, the company adjusts its list of recommendations.

Interactivity also increases customers' sense of being in control, and studies have shown that people who control the flow of information they receive are better able to understand the material they're presented. If your customers are able to give you feedback and ask questions, they'll feel more involved with your business and be more likely to buy your product or service. This type of back-and-forth interaction has caused one expert to describe Web marketing as "a dialogue, as opposed to a monologue, which regular advertising is."

Of course, because Web marketing is a dialogue, it means you need to be very careful in how you conduct your online conversations. The Web has proven to be a very emotional medium in that people seem to feel much more freedom to express anger than they would in face-to-face encounters. This is why you need to be so careful in approaching newsgroups and discussion groups with your promotional materials. If you do it wrong, you'll be roundly flamed—be the target of many angry responses.

Online conversations require you to follow the very special rules of netiquette I presented in Chapter 3. If you've forgotten them, this is a good time to go back and take another look.

IT'S INEXPENSIVE

At its most basic, online marketing is quite inexpensive. If you have a $20-a-month Internet connection and an e-mail account, you have the ability to reach millions. Your setup costs are low, it's easy to update information, and the cost of transmitting information is virtually nil.

Of course, costs do rise with the complexity of your site. But for the small business person, who is selling a limited inventory of items from a site consisting of from ten to twenty pages, the costs are still far below that of a conventional storefront business.

IT'S EASIER TO IDENTIFY MARKETS

The Web has proven to be a medium on which people gather together based on a shared interest. The fact that there are tens of thousands of newsgroups on the Usenet is a perfect example of this behavior. Each group serves as a gathering point where people can post opinions and questions about something important to them. Discussion groups share the same characteristic. For the Web marketer, this behavior provides the same customer data that companies in the physical world pay huge sums of money to obtain.

I hate to use such an unpleasant analogy, but it's like being a hungry lion and finding the gazelles gathered around a water hole. Your targets are right there, ready to be attacked. If you market gardening supplies, all the participants in gardening newsgroups and discussion groups are potential customers. The same is true for music, sporting goods, sailing equipment, and thousands of other items.

As I discussed in the previous chapter, however, you need to be careful how you approach these groups. If you come barging in blindly with your marketing message, you're more than likely going to go down in flames. But if you can establish a presence in a group, either as a participant or as an advertiser whose information is willingly accepted and appreciated, the paybacks can be enormous.

IT ALLOWS RAPID CHANGE

In contrast to other media, the Web allows you to change your marketing message as often as you want for very little cost. For example, you can customize your information to fit the needs of different groups of customers depending on factors such as age, income, sex, and geographic location. Print advertising and direct mail allow you to do this, but to a much lesser degree. It's altogether impossible with broadcast media.

IT'S SEDUCTIVE

Once they're exposed to it, the Web grabs most people in some way or another. That's because there's just so much information available. Some people fall in love with e-mail. Others become addicted to newsgroups or discussion groups. Still others are enthralled by the amount of research information they can find. Many are becoming equally fond of shopping on the Web. As their numbers increase, so will your profits.

IT'S FASTER

No other medium can come close to the speed with which the Web can provide information. For example, you can create a promotional package and, within minutes of completing it, have it sitting in the incoming mail boxes of your customers' e-mail accounts and on your Website.

This is one reason it's important to regularly update the information on your Website. Because information moves so quickly in cyberspace, and there's so much of it, what's news today is old hat a week or two down the road. Web surfers want change, and if you don't provide it, your site will begin to appear stagnant and they'll go elsewhere. If you do provide it, they'll return again and again just to keep up with your news. They're information junkies, and you can manipulate that characteristic to your favor.

The ability to move information at the speed of light also increases your customers' expectations. If someone sends you an e-mail message requesting information or assistance, they'll expect a quick response, as in seconds or minutes. A few hours later, tomorrow, or the next day isn't going to cut it.

It Has Distinct Demographics

The Web audience is generally young, educated, well-paid, and comfortable with technology. Many work for government organizations, colleges and universities, and large corporations. More and more are women. And the fact that companies of all sizes are on the Web is great news for business-to-business marketing, a topic we'll discuss later in the chapter.

It Reaches the Entire World

Or at least those parts of the world that are wired (a percentage that's increasing daily, by the way). It's a market without boundaries, and everyone with an Internet connection is a potential customer. Sitting in his little attic office in Ithaca, New York, Jim Spitznagel has sold compact discs to customers in Europe, Asia, Australia, South America, and even Africa.

IMPORTANT STEPS IN GETTING STARTED

Before you begin marketing your service or product on the Web, you need to ask yourself why you're doing it, how you're going to do it, and what your goals are in doing it. Here are a few things you can do to answer those questions:

LEARN THE LAY OF THE LAND

Get on the Web and analyze as many businesses as you can. Try to think like a consumer. Note what works and what seems like a waste of time. If something really catches your interest, try to figure out why it grabbed you and how you can use the same strategy for your business.

DETERMINE YOUR OBJECTIVES

Your online marketing will augment, not replace, traditional marketing strategies. This is especially true if your Website is an offshoot of a real-world business. Make sure you know what you want your Web marketing campaign to accomplish.

DETERMINE WHAT KIND OF INFORMATION YOU'LL PRESENT

It will need to be complete, able to be quickly absorbed, up-to-date, and stimulating enough to make the customer want to know more and take the appropriate action.

DETERMINE THE STRONG POINTS OF YOUR PRODUCT OR SERVICE

Why should people buy what you're selling? The reasons must be presented right up front, in clear language, and without hyperbole.

DETERMINE WHAT KIND OF RESPONSE YOU WANT

I know what you're thinking. "I want people to visit my site and spend their money, dummy!" But it's really more complex than that. Depending on your product or service, your goal might be simply to have people contact you for information.

DETERMINE WHERE YOU'RE MARKETING

Remember, the Web is a global medium. The same information that's being read by a customer in Venice, California, can be read by a customer in Venice, Italy. Will you be prepared to fulfill orders that come from overseas? We'll look at this issue later in the chapter.

KNOW THE RULES

I've already touched on some of the behavior that can get you in trouble. Here's a more complete list:

Don't send unwanted e-mail. Your e-mail marketing messages should only go to people who have requested information or who have agreed to your request to send them information.

Don't sell consumer information without the consent of your customers. As customers contact you for information about your product or service, you'll compile their names, e-mail addresses, and other information in a data base of prospective customers. This does not give you the right to sell their names to other companies unless they give you permission.

Don't send marketing material to newsgroups or discussion groups unless they permit it. There's nothing more annoying than scrolling through a newsgroup and finding a submission that screams "Make Money Today the Easy Way! Results Guaranteed!" Sending such unwanted advertising to a newsgroup or discussion group will do nothing more than create ill will and result in a massive flaming from unhappy recipients.

Consumer research should only be done with the full consent of the consumer. As we'll discuss, the Web is a wonderful tool for gathering information on your customers. But such information should only be obtained after the consumer is made aware that you're gathering the information for marketing purposes.

Don't conduct promotions without full disclosure to your customers. Special online promotions are fine. But make sure your customers have the chance to read the rules, guidelines, and other information regarding the promotion before they decide to participate.

Don't use your software for purposes that aren't obvious to consumers. The increasing sophistication of Web software and hardware has created concerns among consumers that unscrupulous Web merchants might gather private information from their computers or engage in other kinds of electronic invasions of privacy. Don't do it. At the very least it's unethical. At worst, it may be illegal.

MARKETING STRATEGIES

Thus far, marketing on the Web has been an interesting combination of traditional strategies—either carried out as they have been for years or adjusted to fit into this new medium—and new strategies designed specifically for cyberspace. As we discuss the most common marketing tricks, keep in mind what I pointed out early in the book. This is an industry that's barely on its feet, and what's new today on the Web might be ancient history in six months.

This will be especially true of marketing. Whether in the real world or in cyberspace, it remains the key to business success. A lot of creative minds are hard at work figuring out new ways to reach their customers. Part of your job as a business owner will be to keep an eye on what they're doing. You can't afford to miss out on new ideas.

OFFER INFORMATION AND ADVICE

Store owners in the real world are sources of information to their customers. You can serve the same function by creating an area where customers can e-mail you questions about your product or service. You might consider using the best of the questions you receive to set up a Q & A advice column that your customers can read.

CREATE A COMMUNITY

This kind of interactivity allows businesses to foster the creation of online communities—places where people with shared interests can gather. Let's say you have a compact disc business like Jim Spitznagel's. What's the common interest of all your customers? Music, right? Granted, not everyone is a fan of the same kinds of music. Some may be blues fans. Others might like jazz. Still others may be into reggae or country. But they're all at your site because they share the same general passion.

When I first met Jim, he told me that one of the things he missed about running a storefront business was the interaction with customers and the feedback they would give him. They would ask him to try to find obscure releases or tell him about musicians he had never heard of. For this reason, his shop was more than a place of business. It was a gathering place where people could indulge their love of music and exchange ideas, opinions, and knowledge.

You can create that same kind of environment on your Website by setting up a chat room where people can post queries and opinions. As an expert in the field, you can join in by answering questions and providing information. You can even host special guests for your customers to chat with. I once was the featured guest in an America Online forum on the pros and cons of franchising, which was sponsored by *Small Business Computing* magazine. I sat in my office for an hour while people from all over the country (or the world, for all I know) asked me questions. They appeared in a box on my monitor, and as I answered them, my answers also appeared.

It was quite a novel experience. It also convinced me that this type of "real-time" communication leaves a lot to be desired. When they finally get videoconferencing and audioconferencing perfected for the Web, you'll quickly see the demise of keyboard-generated conversations. It's just too slow and laborious.

When you create this kind of environment, you become much more than just a place of business. You become an environment where people communicate with one another. This increases traffic to your site and goes a long way toward building good-will and consumer awareness of your business.

Conduct Contests

Contests have always been a marketing staple, and they're proving equally popular on the Web, especially as a tool to gather marketing information from consumers. You can give away merchandise, trips, money, and anything else that might grab your customers' attention. Some businesses have new contests every week.

SET UP A GUEST BOOK

Create a guest book where visitors to your site can register. I'll admit this is a not so subtle way of gathering customer data. But it works, so who's to knock it?

GIVE AWAY SAMPLES

The free sample is another marketing staple. If you're like me, you can probably take your family to your local grocery store and enjoy a small meal just by indulging in all the free food items being offered. (You may recall this practice being carried out by Norm Peterson of *Cheers,* who was fond of taking his wife Vera down to Hurley's Market for dinner.)

Web technology makes sampling an equally efficient way to reach customers. The magic of downloading—the transferring of data from a Website to a customer's computer—means you can provide your customers with text, graphics, audio, video, and even software. All they have to do is hit a few buttons. Almost all music companies allow visitors to download samples from recent releases. Similarly, movie studios are making trailers from soon-to-be-released films available over the Web.

Obviously, not all products can be sampled electronically. If you sell garden products, for example, you certainly can't send seeds or fertilizer over the Web. But anyone can send information, no matter what they're selling. And as we learned earlier, Web surfers are information addicts. You might not be able to send your customers seeds, but you can certainly provide them with information on how and when to plant them as well as how to care for the plants they produce.

CREATE A DIRECTORY

The Web is still a confusing place for many people. You can provide travel services for your customers by creating a list of links to sites that are related to your business. For example, if you sell sporting goods, you can create links to the sites of all the professional sports teams and to other sports-related sites.

CREATE A "WHAT'S NEW" LINK

This will keep your customers up-to-date on the latest news from your company. You can announce new products, promotions, contests, and other activities. Remember, though, that news gets old fast on the Web. Update your information often.

JOIN AN ONLINE SHOPPING MALL

Some businesses elect to join online malls as part of their marketing strategy. It's just like having your business in a mall in the physical world. Like a real mall, the traffic generated by the existence of so many businesses means more traffic for each individual business. Also like a real mall, each business pays for its space.

Here's what you get for your money:

Publicity and Advertising

The mall operator will be responsible for generating publicity and advertising for its member businesses. The idea is that as more consumers visit the mall, traffic to each business will increase. Some malls are operated by high-profile companies such as MCI. The added "name brand" recognition can help attract customers.

Security and Shopping Procedures

Most electronic malls also take care of the security of their businesses' online transactions, which serves to lessen the fears of nervous online shoppers. They may also provide streamlined shopping services such as shopping carts and other features.

Experience and Expertise

Most mall operators are savvy Web entrepreneurs with a great deal of experience in both Website design and online transactions. They use their expertise to provide services to their "tenants."

Customized Services

The more sophisticated malls may offer services that match customer interests with the merchandise offered by member businesses. For your customers, it's like having a kind of "personal shopper" who can direct them to the kind of merchandise they favor. This is another of the wonderful tools that the interactivity of the Web provides.

Most online mall operators charge participating businesses a portion of their gross sales. Is the expense worth it? It depends on whether or not you depend entirely on the mall operator to generate your business. If you do, then he's entitled to a piece of all the action. But if you conduct your own marketing and advertising efforts as well, you're going to have a hard time coming to terms with the arrangement.

There are a number of online malls out there. Contact their operators and comparison shop. It really comes down to return on investment. If being a member of a mall brings more traffic to your site and increases sales, it can be a good arrangement. You also need to consider the additional services the mall operator may provide, such as expertise he can offer you and the customized assistance he can provide your customers.

To get an idea of how online malls operate, take a look at these mall sites:

➡ **American Shopping Mall** (*http://www.greenearth.com*)
➡ **Shopnow.com** (*http://www.shopnow.com/*)
➡ **eMall** (*http://www.emall.com*)
➡ **InternetPlaza** (*http://storefront.xor.com/index.html*)
➡ **Shopsite** (*http://www.shopsite.com*)

KEEP YOUR CUSTOMERS FOCUSED WITH MICROSITES

One of the risks run by Web businesses is they can become so large that they become cumbersome to navigate. This, in turn, can make important information difficult to find. As a solution, some Web businesses are creating what are called "microsites" to feature new products, conduct promotional campaigns, or host other information.

A microsite is a Website unto itself, with its own URL. The advantage of microsites is that they can be tailored for a specific purpose. They follow the lead of Hollywood film marketing, which creates a new Website for each film that's released rather than requiring people to link to the film from the studio's site.

How can a microsite help your business? Let's say you have a new product you're excited about. A customer picks up some promotional literature on the product and is directed to your Website. But once he logs on he may have trouble finding the information he wants, particularly if the link to that information hasn't been given a prominent enough location on your home page. You'll not only have lost a potential sale, you'll have discouraged the customer from visiting your site in the future.

A microsite devoted solely to the new product avoids this problem. By publicizing the site's URL with promotional literature for your new product, you direct customers to the microsite, which, of course, is linked to your primary Website. In addition to new product information, microsites can be used for any situation in which important, detailed information needs to be made available quickly and easily. The microsite can be temporary, with a life span that lasts only as long as the event it's advertising.

BUSINESS-TO-BUSINESS MARKETING

Business-to-business marketing is still the dominant segment of Web marketing. It's only natural since so many of the earliest users of the Internet and the Web were businesses. It didn't take them long to realize they could save an enormous amount of money on sales literature and promotional material by setting up Websites. Many were also able to reduce the size of their sales forces, which added to their savings.

If you have a product or service that you sell to other businesses, the Web is a powerful marketing tool that you must use. If you don't, quite frankly, you're missing the boat. The Web not only makes marketing easier, it makes buying easier. If a company can get the same product from you or one of your competitors, and your competitor has a Website and you don't, you're going to lose the sale, pure and simple. Time is money in the business world, and buying products over the Web saves time.

When you're creating a Website to market to businesses, think about the kind of information you as a business owner want to see from your suppliers. Use that as the foundation for your site. Explain what your company does, the products it offers, and why your products are superior to those of your competitors. Explain the advantages you can offer your customers and how you'll provide them. Include detailed descriptions of your products and services, prices, and ordering information. Make sure your e-mail address, phone numbers, and fax numbers are prominently displayed. If you're contacted for information, reply *immediately.*

Don't forget the story of the satisfied customer, which is another longstanding marketing strategy. You can use your Website to describe a few case studies—examples where your product or service helped a company achieve a certain goal or solve a problem. It's also critical that you list your site with commercial indexes and have links to industry-related "hub sites," which we'll talk about later in the chapter.

Here are a few sites that can be helpful to business-to-business marketers. If you have a business that sells to businesses, you'll also need to make sure your URL is included on these sites:

➡ **BizWeb** (*http://www.bizweb.com*) This is a list of more than 40,000 companies in 192 industries. It includes links to their Websites.
➡ **WebTrack** (*http://www.webtrack.com*) This site contains a large list of companies that accept advertising on their Websites.
➡ **Open Market** (*http://www.directory.net*) This is a list of more than 23,000 links to companies offering all sorts of products and services. You can view the lists by category or conduct a search.

INTERNATIONAL MARKETING

This is a fuzzy area for a lot of Web entrepreneurs. Your Website will be visited by people around the world, so you'll need to be able to process orders from people from other countries. If you don't, it will cost you money. Studies have found that an alarming number of Web entrepreneurs have actually ignored overseas orders because they weren't prepared to handle such transactions.

It's true that at the moment the United States and Canada account for the majority of the world's Web users. But that's quickly changing, and new developments on the Web are beginning to take into account the language and cultural considerations presented by this growing audience. Many corporations that do business worldwide are now creating duplicate Websites, or at least certain parts of their Websites, in Spanish, French, German, and other languages.

This issue will continue to receive a great deal of attention as the Web continues to reach around the world. For the moment, here's some advice from marketing experts on how you can prepare to do business internationally.

- Determine which countries are viable markets for your product or service.

- Register your site with search engines in those countries. This will allow potential customers to find you with greater ease.

- Provide all pertinent product, ordering, and payment information—including shipping costs—in the language of those countries. Granted, many customers will be able to conduct transactions in English, but can you afford to lose the business of those who can't? Use e-mail to promptly acknowledge orders and provide shipping information.

- Learn the requirements for international shipping and set up your order fulfillment operation to meet those requirements.

COPYWRITING FOR THE WEB

The Web is becoming an increasingly crowded place. Just as in the physical world, your ads are going to be competing with thousands and thousands of other ads for your customers' attention. So, just as in the physical world, your ad copy has one mission—to grab people. Once it grabs them, it has to entice them to your site.

GET YOUR CUSTOMERS' ATTENTION QUICKLY

When Websites are opening on a customer's monitor, text will appear before any graphics. This is when your grabber needs to do its job. It can be a word or it can be a short phrase. Whatever it is, it has to appear quickly and make the customer think, "Whoa! This looks good. I think I'll hang around and see what this is all about."

Placement on the page is also critical. If your page requires the customer to scroll down to view it in its entirety, the grabber must appear above the scrolling area. If it's not, it won't be seen until the customer scrolls down the page. By that time its effectiveness will be severely diluted.

BREAK UP YOUR COPY

There's nothing wrong with having a lot of copy on your site. But containing it in one endless block is a sure way to send your customers fleeing in droves. Try it yourself. Find a site where the copy goes on endlessly. They're not hard to find. I'll guarantee that your eyes will glaze over before you've even begun reading.

Keep your copy organized in small blocks that your customers can easily digest. Each block should contain information on a single topic. Keep your sentences short and to the point. People on the Web want information and they want it quickly. They're not interested in flowery prose.

USE BULLETED LISTS

Bulleted lists are even better than short copy blocks because they're easier to read. They should be used any time you have

a sequence of information, such as a list of products or a series
of instructions. Your customers will thank you for it.

DON'T GET OFF THE TOPIC

Keep to the point. Every sentence you write and every headline
you use should serve to keep the customer's attention and interest levels as high as possible. To do otherwise is to risk losing
a sale.

DIFFERENT PRODUCTS REQUIRE DIFFERENT STYLES

Having said all that, I'll also point out that certain products can
benefit from a little more style in the copy. Generally, any
product that appeals to the ego—clothing, cars, gourmet foods—
can use a bit of polished text. Customers need a little stroking
to assure them the product will help them achieve their desired image.

But if the product is more utilitarian—tools, office products,
software—the copy should be equally utilitarian. Say what it is
and what it does and leave it at that.

CONDUCTING MARKET RESEARCH

There has never been a better tool for conducting market research than the World Wide Web. Compared to the cost of data
collection in the physical world, research on the Web costs next
to nothing. And not only does the technology make it easy to
collect information, it also allows you to conduct extremely
personalized marketing campaigns based on the demographic
characteristics of different groups of customers.

Here are the best ways small businesses can conduct market
research on the Web:

SOLICIT INFORMATION

The interactivity of the Web makes it a great research tool. You
can ask questions of people and be certain most of them will

provide you with an answer. There's something about e-mail and the ability to remain anonymous to others that inspires people to be quite frank in their online communications.

One way to gather consumer information is to include a survey on your Website and ask visitors to answer the questions. You can do random e-mail surveys, which is like doing a telephone survey. It's even possible to do focus groups online, using a discussion list.

TRADE FOR INFORMATION

Some people won't be willing to provide you information for free. But they might agree to participate if you dangle a gift in front of them. This type of arrangement is becoming increasingly common on the Web. The enticement might be the chance to win a prize in a drawing, discounted merchandise, or even free merchandise. Some businesses offer access to news or information. In return, you'll be provided with names, e-mail addresses, demographic data, and opinions on products or services.

You might also be able to trade information with other Web businesses. There are many customer overlaps if you look for them, and if the other businesses are not in direct competition with you, it can be an advantage to you both.

Let's use an online golf equipment business as an example again. It's safe to assume that all your customers are golfers. Then let's look at an online travel agent who, among his many travel packages, sells golf vacations. I think it's safe to assume that all his customers are also golfers.

I smell a deal cooking here, don't you? You each have a data base of customers with the same interests, and you're not competing against each other. To use a tired expression, it's a win-win situation. I'll show you mine if you show me yours.

Once again, however, I'll add that critical caveat about privacy. When people provide information to Web marketers, there may or may not be an understanding that the information is confidential. If there is, that confidentiality must be respected.

Buy Information

This is obviously the least attractive approach, but it could be worth the investment. Buying and selling customer information has for years been a staple of the mail order business. Such lists have equal value on the Web. But as with trading lists, confidentiality must be respected.

THE PRIVACY ISSUE

We've already discussed one important aspect of Web privacy—the concern over the security of credit card numbers used to make online transactions. But that has as much to do with security as privacy. And in any event, it's just one part of a much broader picture.

I've already mentioned this several times, but I'll point it out once more. For many people, one of the most appealing aspects of the Web is the ability to be anonymous. You can interact with thousands of people to whom you're nothing more than a sequence of letters and numbers. You can say whatever you want. You can purchase things you'd be unlikely to purchase in the physical world (it's no coincidence that pornography is a boom industry on the Web). You can even pretend to be someone you're not. And it's all because you can operate in total anonymity.

But as the Web increasingly becomes a business environment, there are going to be a lot of people who want to get as much information as they can about as many people as they can, and that has a lot of people worried. There are a number of organizations looking real hard at privacy issues on the Web in the hope of creating standards that will allow people to remain as faceless as they want.

A lot of the concern is over data-gathering efforts like those we just discussed. It's apparent that people don't want information about their personal lives sold and bartered all over the Web. The level of concern was vividly illustrated when America Online subscribers rose up in protest when they learned the company intended to sell its subscriber information (the company backed off). Consumers may be told that the information they provide a marketer is confidential, but they have no way of knowing if that's really the case. The next thing they know, they could be bombarded with unwanted come-ons from companies that have purchased their information.

YOUR RESPONSIBILITY

The best thing you as a Web merchant can do is be honest. If you're seeking customer information, tell respondents what you intend to do with it. Keep your data confidential and use it to create better service and to facilitate communication between you and your customers. To treat the information in any other manner is a disservice to your customers and can cause a great deal of harm to your business.

A SOLUTION MAY BE NEAR

Just as it has with the security issue, the economic potential of the Web has companies and organizations scrambling to come up with a solution to the privacy issue. The answer may be a proposed standard called the Open Profiling Standard (OPS). First proposed by Netscape and a few other companies, the idea now has the endorsement of the Federal Trade Commission and the Electronic Privacy Information Center and has been submitted to Tim Berners-Lee's World Wide Web Consortium for study. Just how much money is at stake? Well, Microsoft and Netscape are working together on the system. That should tell you something.

The OPS would be like a nationwide electronic identity program. It would allow each person to create an electronic profile of themselves that would be recognized by all the servers on the Internet. The profile only has to be completed once, the user can control what's contained in the profile, and the information can be changed at any time.

If it works—and it should, considering the clout that's backing it up—OPS will go a long way toward solving the privacy issue. Using it with the Secure Electronic Transaction Protocol (SET) described in Chapter 7 should make shopping in cyberspace more secure than ever before. And that should bring more customers to your electronic storefront.

For information on privacy and other issues facing the Internet, take a look at these sites:

➡ **Center for Democracy and Technology** (*http://www.cdt.org*)
➡ **Electronic Frontier Foundation** (*http://www.eff.org*)
➡ **Electronic Privacy Information Center** (*http://www.epic.org*)
➡ **National Consumers League** (*http://www.natlconsumers league.org*)
➡ **World Wide Web Consortium** (*http://www.w3.org*)

LEGAL ISSUES

At the moment, the Web is a hornet's nest of legal issues, and it's likely to remain that way for some time. This is because the Web is literally a new world, and trying to apply some of the same rules that exist in the physical world to cyber issues is extremely difficult. There are so many questions being examined, it's hard to keep up with them all.

A good example of the confusion is the failure of the Communications Decency Act. Created by Congress as a way to keep pornographic materials off the Web, the act was overturned in 1997 in a decision based largely on the First Amendment. There's no question it was a valid decision. Free speech certainly is as much of a right on the Web as it is in the rest of the world. But it also points out the fact that dealing with such issues in cyberspace is going to require a whole new perspective.

A lot of the problem is the ease with which information can be accessed. If you've spent any time at all surfing the Web, you've no doubt discovered that once you're online, you're only a dozen or so keystrokes away from some pretty raunchy stuff. Kids know this, too, and it's an enormous concern. In the real world, twelve-year-olds can't get into an adult bookstore. On the Web, they can browse around literally hundreds of digital adult bookstores to their hearts' content.

Lawmakers will continue to struggle with this issue, as they will with issues of privacy and the sale of personal information. As a businessperson on the Web, you'll need to monitor these legal developments and make sure they're reflected in the way you run your business.

THE COPYRIGHT ISSUE

This is a good time to bring up another thorny issue. All material you create for your Website, including the site itself, is protected by copyright law. This means you have the sole rights to its use. If someone else should use it, they're in violation of the law and liable for damages. If you should use material created by someone else, including written copy or images, *you're* the one who's breaking the law and can be sued.

Once again, it's the nature of this new environment that's caused so much confusion. Consider this scenario. Let's say you've created your own Website—not for your business but for yourself. This has proven to be a hugely popular practice among Web enthusiasts. Most people include all sorts of information about themselves (that absolutely no one but them cares about). They'll tell you about their interests and hobbies and create links to their favorite sites. They'll include pictures of their pets and their cars and their houses. So far, so good.

But then they'll do things like put favorite cartoon strips on their sites. Or photos they've scanned from books or magazines. Or other stuff they've culled from various sources. As soon as they do that, they're in violation of copyright law, and technically they could be sued. The guy who draws the comic strip "Dilbert" could have a field day tracking down people who have included his strips on their Websites (as if he needs the money).

Keep this in mind when you're putting material on your site. Make sure it's original. If it's not, you need to obtain permission from the person or company that holds the rights to it.

To protect your own material, you can attach a copyright notice to your Website. Some sites just put a copyright notice on their home page. Others put one on every page in the site. My advice? Do the latter to avoid any confusion. If you include material that you want people to download, which is certainly a good possibility since you're running a business, you need to denote that as well.

A copyright must include three things: the word "copyright" or the copyright symbol ©, the year the material was created, and the name of the person holding the copyright. It's not a bad idea to add the phrase "All rights reserved." If you intend for people to copy the material, you can add a phrase that says "This material may be copied and distributed subject to inclusion of this copyright notice."

ADVERTISING STRATEGIES ON THE WEB

Just as with marketing strategies, advertising on the Web has a few unique twists. The way advertising is created, delivered, and received by consumers are all quite different from traditional advertising. We'll begin by looking at some figures.

ONLINE ADVERTISING IS BOOMING

A quick look at advertising trends on the Web should erase any doubts that the Web is coming into its own as a place to conduct business. In 1995, online advertising revenues totaled just $37 million. They jumped to $260 million in 1996 and more than $850 million in 1997. And although the final figures for 1998 had not been tabulated as this book was being written, a survey by the Internet Advertising Bureau noted that the total for just the first three-quarters of the year had already passed *$1 billion*. Third quarter revenues alone were $491 million, an increase of 116 percent from 1997. Analysts were comparing Web advertising trends to those in traditional media, noting the same kinds of seasonal ups and downs. They also predicted a 250 percent annual growth in advertising spending through the year 2000.

It was also becoming apparent that the return on advertising investment was improving. A 1997 study commissioned by the

Direct Marketing Association reported that returns on Internet advertising spending had nearly doubled since 1994. According to the study, every dollar spent to advertise in cyberspace that year generated seven dollars in sales. In 1994, the figure was four dollars.

The study was one of the first of its kind to measure the influence that direct marketing has had on electronic commerce. It reported that the five leading industries to use direct marketing to generate sales in 1997 were business services, computers, communications, office equipment, and printing and publishing.

GATEWAY ADS

Gateway ads, which are really just links that look like tiny billboards, take customers directly to your home page. They're becoming the most common form of advertising on the Web. Their appearance is usually as a graphic—frequently in an elongated horizontal box called a "banner"—that customers click on to be sent to the advertiser's Website. Gateway ads are unobtrusive (most of them, anyway) and allow the customer to decide whether or not he wants to visit your site. They are proving to be an extremely effective means of attracting customers to businesses, and will no doubt continue to be for the foreseeable future.

How Do Gateway Ads Work?

It's really quite simple. Once you purchase advertising space from another Website, your ad will appear at the agreed upon location in the site. As I mentioned in Chapter 8, most ads share space with a number of other ads and take turns appearing as new visitors view a certain page. The most common banner size is a screen-wide, inch-high strip. Other banners have a variety of dimensions, including the entire page.

Creating a Gateway Ad

Gateway ads will be a direct road to your Website, so you want to do everything you can to make sure people click on them.

The design and copy will determine whether people are intrigued enough to pay you a visit or whether they choose to ignore you.

Everything must be considered. What's the best size for the ad? Where should it appear on the page? What kind of image should be used? What should the copy say? How much copy should there be? Will there be other ads on the same page that draw attention away from yours?

At this point the most critical decision is probably size. Your ad should be big enough to be noticed but not so large as to be obnoxious. The inch-high, screen-wide format has evolved as the most common size because it meets both these criteria. But you can make ads bigger or smaller. You can even make them full-screen and, if the site you're buying space from agrees, require that visitors pass through the ad in order to move further into the site. Whether this kind of "forced viewing" is a good strategy for both the advertiser and the business providing the space remains to be seen.

Strategies for Gateway Ads

Gateway ads are still evolving. What works and what doesn't is still a matter of debate. But here are some of the current strategies:

Use an action-oriented approach. Make your message active to create greater customer interest. For example, if you're selling golf equipment, your ad should say something like, "Take strokes off your game!!" rather than a more banal message like, "See this season's new equipment."

Generate an emotion. A good ad creates excitement, curiosity, wonder, or a sense of mystery. This is why the last thing you should do is just have your logo or the name of your business sitting there. Yawn.

Change your ad regularly. A fresh approach keeps customers coming back. Don't let your ad get stagnant. And don't be afraid to experiment with bold colors and unusual typefaces.

Publicize new products or promotions. Let customers know there's something new behind the ad.

Targeting Your Customers

As I mentioned before, one of the great advantages of the Web over traditional advertising mediums is that it allows you to cost-effectively target many different audiences. You can create ads specifically for women, specifically for men, or for a specific age group within a certain gender. You can create ads aimed at butchers who live in the Northeast, bakers who live in the Northwest, and candlestick makers who live in Europe. No demographic group, no matter how small, is beyond your reach.

One common strategy is to buy ad space in the kind of sites your target demographic group is most likely to visit. If you sell golf equipment, buy ad space in golf-related sites. If you sell sailing gear, advertise in sites related to sailing. Another strategy is to fashion your message to appeal to your target audience. The appearance of your ad and the copy it contains can be fine-tuned to attract the attention of the customers you're most trying to reach.

Gateway Ad Prices

There is as yet no fixed method for determining the prices of gateway ads. Some sites will charge a fixed price based on monthly or quarterly rates. For the potential advertiser, this makes it easy to compare the value of the service to the price. If you decide you're not getting the desired response from your ad, you don't renew your contract.

Some sites guarantee that a certain number of people will see the ad. Each viewing is called an "impression" or an "exposure" in Web lingo. They base their fees on "cost per thousand" impressions (CPM). Other sites sell rotating ads where the space is shared by different businesses and each business is guaranteed that their ad will appear a certain number of times each week. As I mentioned at the end of Chapter 8, you can now buy a rotating banner ad on some search engines for around $1,000 a week. Yahoo!, for example, guarantees 120,000 impressions each week for ads in that price range.

Of course, having people see the ad (an "impression") and having them click on it to visit your site (a "click-through") are two different things. That's why some sites charge their advertisers a "per click" fee. If no one visits your site, you don't pay. According to statistical analyses of Web behavior, from 2 to 3.5 percent of the people who see your banner will click on it.

Where Should You Place Your Gateway Ads?

The Web is a big place, and every site that's on it is a potential advertising space. Here are some of your options:

Search engines and directories. It's no coincidence that search engines and directories have enjoyed the most revenue from advertisers thus far. They reach an enormous audience, and because they break down sites by category, they can strategically place your ad so the majority of people who see it have an interest in your product or service. Just remember one thing: the more specific the category in which you place your ad, the more you'll pay. The people who run these things aren't dummies. Because of their prices, which can run from $25 to $40 CPM, search engines and directories are only for businesses that can afford a few thousand dollars a month in advertising costs. They're not realistic for most small businesses.

Secondary high traffic sites. After the search engines and directories, the sites with the largest traffic volume on the Web are those of news and entertainment organizations such as CNN, Sony Pictures, ESPN, and USA Today. Prices will be a little cheaper than those of search engines, usually in the $15 to $30 CPM range, but high enough to keep them out of reach of a lot of small businesses.

Smaller focused content sites. These sites focus on a specific industry or theme, such as real estate or insurance or sports. Although their prices can be somewhat less than the first two options, many will still be quite pricey, as high as $50 or $60 CPM. This is because they have fewer visitors and therefore can sell fewer impressions than the high traffic sites. They need to charge more to make a profit. On the other hand, although they're more expensive, they also provide you with an audience in which every visitor is a potential customer.

Local sites. This is the logical choice for small service-based businesses whose clientele is limited to a certain geographic area. Many community newspapers today have Websites, as do local organizations. In fact, there are quite a few *communities* that have Websites. For the small local business owner, they can be an effective and affordable place to advertise.

Metascreens. This a relatively new idea in the banner ad world. A metascreen is a full-page banner ad that will appear when a visitor opens a site. It will remain there for five seconds to a half a minute before disappearing, allowing the viewer to enter the site. Many metascreens, particularly the longer ones, are quite sophisticated and use animation and other sophisticated tricks. The jury is still very much out on this type of banner ad. Companies run the obvious risk that consumers will be put off by being forced to sit through something they're not particularly interested in. Web surfers are used to having control over where they go and what they do. Metascreens hold them prisoner. My gut feeling is that this idea will need a little fine-tuning if it's really going to work. A good indication of this is the response of a friend of mine, an experienced Web surfer, when I described what would happen if she encountered a metascreen. "The hell with that," she snorted. "I'd hit the back button and get outta Dodge. And I'd never come back."

Join a Link Exchange

Here's a way you can try out different ads for free. A link exchange is a group of businesses that agree to host each other's gateway ads. Dozens of businesses will take turns putting your ad on their site. In return, you'll put a rotating banner with various ads on your site. This gives everyone involved the opportunity to try out different ads and monitor the responses to each one.

Using an Advertising Broker

Another option is to use the services of an advertising broker to help you find the best places to place your ads. Brokers represent sites in return for a commission. The best brokers will have the expertise to help you make solid decisions. The worst won't have a clue but will try to convince you otherwise. They'll try to tell you they can pick sites where you'll get ten times the industry average in click-through rates, or they'll tell you other tall tales. Brokers can be worth your trouble. Just be careful who you're dealing with.

Testing Your Gateway Ad

Once you've placed an ad, you'll be anxious to find out if it's working or not. All you have to do is contact your ISP, who will keep a traffic log that tells you how many people visit your site every day and what pages they visit. If you don't notice an immediate and significant increase in traffic to your site, you can do one of two things: redesign your ad, or let your contract with the advertiser expire and try your luck somewhere else.

This brings me to an important point. For obvious reasons, you should keep your initial contract with an advertising site as short as possible. That way, if the ad doesn't work out, you'll be able to get out quickly and cut your losses. If you find that advertising at the site provides a good response, you can commit to a longer contract.

Hubsites

This might be thought of as the "If you want to play with the big dogs, you have to go where the big dogs hang out" approach to advertising. Hubsites are industry-specific Websites that serve as launching pads to the sites of businesses, professionals, and associations in the industry they represent. In that sense, they really function as directories. They make it easier for customers to find businesses.

Some hubsites charge a fee for including your business in their lists and creating a link to it. Others rely on advertising revenues to make money. Some offer Website design services. They also facilitate business-to-business transactions.

LAUNCHING AN ONLINE AD CAMPAIGN

All advertising experts will agree on one thing: advertising is an inexact science in which the reason for one ad's success and another's failure is often a total mystery. They're just happy they sometimes get it right.

Things are basically the same on the Web, but with one important difference—you have much more versatility. Online ads are different from ads in the physical world. Those cost huge sums of money and live or die on their own merits once they're placed in a magazine or newspaper or inserted into a broadcast schedule. Online ads, on the other hand, can be easily changed during their life span on an advertising site. If the numbers from your ISP aren't bringing down the house, you can fine-tune to your heart's content until you either get it right or you exhaust all the impressions you've contracted for.

Here are some of the considerations in creating an effective online ad campaign:

IDENTIFY YOUR AUDIENCE

All businesses need to know exactly who the audience is for their products and services. If you've been conducting your business in the real world, you'll already have the answer. If your cyberbusiness is a brand new venture, however, this audience must be clearly defined before you begin any advertising plans.

Your target audience must be broken down by sex, age, education, occupation, income, location, interests, and other categories that will help you effectively target your advertising. These can then be matched to the target profiles developed by specific Websites that sell advertising.

You can also target groups based on the information contained in e-mail addresses or URLs. Some advertising sites are using software that will display your ad only when a visitor's information matches your target group. For example, suppose you have a product aimed at college students. When a customer with ".edu" in their e-mail address arrives at the site, your ad would then appear.

FINE-TUNE YOUR BANNER

Defining your audience will help you fine-tune your message to attract customers. It begins with your banner. Web surfers move quickly, clicking from one site to another as fast as their fingers will let them. Your banner's job is to get them to slam on the brakes and take a closer look. What will do it? The proper message delivered through a combination of words and images.

Some Web marketers compare the banner to the envelope that contains direct mail marketing materials, with the Website being the materials themselves. Or you might consider the banner the door and the Website as your store. Once the customer has come through the door, so to speak, the rest is up to the design of the site itself.

To do its job, your banner has to accomplish the first rule of the four rules of influencing customer behavior preached by direct mail professionals: *get attention.* The other three rules are *arouse interest, stimulate desire,* and *generate action.* Those are the tasks of your Website. Here are several ways your banner can get attention:

Download Early

The quicker something appears on a page, the more attention it will get. Studies have shown that banners appearing prominently on the first page of a site have the highest click-through rates.

Make It Big

Studies have also found that the larger the banner, the higher its click-through rate. The only problem is that banner size is usually out of your control. Most sites don't allow their advertisers a choice of sizes. This means you may find a site that has great potential as an advertising vehicle for your product, but you might have to reject it if you feel its banner sizes are too small. Customer demand, however, may result in more advertisers offering a variety of sizes.

Experiment with Text, Graphics, and Color

Unfortunately, there's no magic formula for determining what combination of text, graphics, and color will prove most stimulating to your customers. The good news is you can experiment. Link exchanges are a great tool for trying out your ad before you make a major commitment to an advertiser. You can also begin with short contracts that allow you to monitor the ad's effectiveness. And don't forget that you can tinker with an ad constantly, even when it's on an advertiser's site.

Use Different Ads

If you have ads at different sites, you may want to make them different from each other. This flies in the face of some advertising strategies in traditional media, which will place the same ad in a variety of venues. But once again, cyberspace is different. Your mission is to get people to click on the banner, so you may have better luck with a variety of banners than just one. Using different banners also allows you to compare click-through rates. If you find that some ads are dramatically outperforming others, you can expand your use of the effective ads and dump the ineffective ones.

PROPER AD PLACEMENT

There are three criteria you should use in selecting an advertising site: audience, visitor rate, and value. The site's audience should match the demographic profile of your customers. The visitor rate should be a minimum of 10,000 visitors a month. And the price should fit within your budget and be based on CPM.

Are there good deals out there? You bet. Advertising rates are a long way from being carved in stone, and many new sites will keep their rates low to attract advertisers. You can even find established, high-traffic sites that offer reasonable rates.

Many companies now include their advertising rates, demographic data, and other advertising information as pages on their sites. Others will provide it on request. A company's rate card should include the number of visitors it receives daily, weekly, or monthly; the number of hits it receives daily, weekly, or monthly; the number of subscribers it has (if applicable); and its rates, based on either CPM or click-through. If the company offers volume discount rates or agency/broker discounts, that information should be included.

A site that provides really good customer service—unfortunately, not many fall into this category—will also include detailed demographic data on its visitors. It will have percentages of both sexes, ages, income levels, occupation profiles, and even what companies or organizations are represented. It will also include extensive information on itself, including the company that owns the site (this is not always obvious), when the site was created, and any awards or recognition it has received.

COMPARING COSTS

Costs are all over the place. Perhaps the only universal rule of thumb is that the more impressions you contract for, the lower the CPM. Some large sites will charge as little as $3 per CPM, an incredibly cheap rate. The catch? You might have to agree to as many as twenty million impressions. That's a $60,000 commitment, and one that most small advertisers cannot afford (or need, for that matter).

The best deals are smaller, focused-content sites that fall within the lower end of their price range ($30-$80 CPM). Because these sites are so narrowly focused—dealing with a particular industry or activity—almost all their visitors are potential customers.

The bottom line with Web advertising is pretty much like that of any other purchase—you have to find the best deal for your money. Compare costs with services and go with what you think is the best deal. If it doesn't work out to your satisfaction, look for other advertisers.

AD EXCHANGES

Ah, the beauty of the barter system. If you can find other businesses whose customers are likely customers for your product or service, but with whom you're not in direct competition, hosting each other's ads is the perfect strategy. Think back to the golf shop/golf travel agent deal I mentioned earlier in the chapter. There are any number of potential relationships that can work in this manner. It just requires a little thought to figure them out.

BUYING KEYWORDS

This is an extremely effective—but more costly—method of displaying your banner. You can buy the right to "keywords" that are likely to be used by customers doing a search for your product. Your ad would then only appear when one of those keywords is entered. Let's use the golf shop example again. You might buy the right to "golf clubs," "golf balls," or just "golf." When those words are entered, your banner would appear.

The downside to this strategy is the cost. Keyword advertising can be twice as expensive as just having your banner appear at random on a rotating ad. But consider what you're getting for your money. If you have the right product and select the right words, every person who sees your banner is a qualified buyer. Exposure to such an extremely focused audience just might be worth the extra money.

Do You Need an Ad Agency?

Any business can benefit from the services of an experienced advertising or marketing professional. So the answer is yes, if you can afford one.

The key word here is "experienced." As I've pointed out so many times in this book, this is a new business environment and it's turned many traditional ways of doing business upside down. The person or agency you hire must have experience in marketing and advertising on the Web. Ask for references and samples of their work. If they haven't done any work in cyberspace, look elsewhere, no matter how highly recommended they come.

FINE-TUNING YOUR AD CAMPAIGN

No other form of advertising can provide you with the kind of feedback you get from the Web. Because it can give you information on both the success of your advertising efforts and the audience you're reaching, your ads, your copy, the images you use, and every other facet of your ad campaign can be fine-tuned almost daily.

This is all made possible by the sheer volume of numbers gathered by various data-keeping programs on the Web. Your ISP will gather numbers, as will online audit bureaus, commercial statistics gatherers, and your Web advertiser. You can even buy software programs that will compile data into extremely useful charts and graphs that paint an accurate picture of the kind of traffic your ad campaign is generating.

Here are the most important sources of data:

ISP Reports

Most ISP servers use a "common log format" (CLF) that enters information about each visitor to your site into a kind of electronic ledger. Among other things, it will tell you what kind of domain they belong to (.edu, .org, .net, .com, for example), the date and time they visited your site, whether they entered data (as in an order for merchandise) or retrieved data (opened a page) while they were there, and the size of the files they retrieved.

What can you glean from this kind of information? All sorts of things. The domain information will tell you a lot about your visitors—whether they're from colleges and universities, nonprofits, government organizations, or arriving at your site through other ISPs. The date and time of visits will indicate, among other things, traffic peaks and valleys at your site and whether there is the desired increase in visits after you start various ad campaigns. The activity record can tell you if a lot of files on your site are being opened or if visitors are just taking a quick look at your home page and then heading elsewhere.

What Are Hits, Anyway?

This is a good time to discuss "hits," since they seem to be the criteria by which many people mistakenly measure a site's popularity. There's some confusion about what constitutes a hit. Many people think that one hit is equivalent to one visit to a site.

Wrong.

A hit represents the transfer of a file of information from a server to a browser. The file can be a piece of text, a graphic, or anything else constructed from bits of data. For example, to get to your home page, a customer must either type your URL into his browser or hit a link or bookmark for your site. At that point all the files that go together to create your home page are sent from your ISP's server—the home of your Website—to the customer's browser. If there are a dozen files, it counts as a dozen hits. Each subsequent page the customer opens creates more hits as the files are transferred to his browser. A single visitor to your site can generate hundreds of hits in just a few minutes.

So, as you can see, hits are not a good measure of the number of visitors to your site. This is why terms like "impression" or "view" or even "visit" have come into favor. What hits are a good measure of, however, is overall activity at your site.

If the records from your ISP indicate that most visitors to your Website are spending a lot of time rummaging around, and creating a lot of hits in the process, it's a good sign they find the site interesting. It's when they show up, take one look at your home page, and then head off into the void that you have to start worrying.

The Cookie Controversy

Cookies are another method used to gather data on the Web. They've caused a bit of a furor, so much so, in fact, that many browsers now have an option that lets people know when they've encountered a cookie.

A cookie (the origin of the name is a mystery) is a small file that can be passed back and forth between a browser and a person's computer. They were originally designed with the best of intentions. Netscape, for example, uses cookies as a service to people who use the Netscape browser. It installs a cookie on each user's hard drive that stores their password and user name. Then, when the user wants to log onto Netscape, all he has to do is click on the Netscape icon rather than log on manually.

Cookies are also often the shopping carts that facilitate online shopping (we'll take a closer look at shopping carts in the next chapter). They allow a server to keep track of the selections being made by multiple shoppers. Each customer's selections are stored on a cookie in the computer and then retrieved when the customer is ready to check out. At that point the information is presented as a page listing all the items the customer has selected and the total cost.

The problem is that cookies can also gather much more information than just your password and user name. This includes the Websites you visit—information you may want kept confidential. Because of the data they gather, cookies can also be used to create user profiles. This is the reason they've become part of the privacy debate.

To keep their users happy, Netscape and other browsers have installed cookie alerts that, when activated, let customers know when a merchant's server wants to install a cookie on their computers. This can be a problem in servicing your customers. If they don't allow the cookie to be set, it will disable your shopping cart. If you use cookies for your shopping cart service, you should explain that to customers on your home page. You should also indicate to your customers whether or not you use cookies to gather information about them.

CLICK-THROUGH RATES

Click-through rates tell you what percentage of people who see your banner ad click on it. You might be surprised at how few visitors bother to take a look at your site. The average click-through rate cited by most studies ranges from 2 to 3 percent. It's slightly higher in foreign countries, which may be explained by the novelty of the Web overseas. It's even higher, from 3 to 8 percent, when banner ads include freebies, contests, or special promotions.

PUTTING YOUR INFORMATION TO WORK

All this information allows you to fine-tune your banner ads and other advertising messages. Most advertisers will let you change your ad at least once a week. Web exchanges usually allow a change every two or three days. So the opportunity is there to do a lot of tinkering.

Don't jump to any conclusions about an ad's effectiveness. You should wait until an ad has had at least 300 impressions before you take a look at the click-through rate. You're even better off waiting until 400 or 500 people have had a look at your ad.

You may find you get significantly different click-through rates on different sites. This is quite common and makes sense if you think about it. Different sites draw people from different demographic groups. Comparing the click-through rate with the CPM of a site will help you determine if your advertising dollars are being wisely spent at that site.

IT'S AN ONGOING JOB

After wading through this chapter, it's important that we finish with one very important point. This new commercial environment is just getting off the ground. Some Web experts say that three months on the Web is equivalent to a year in the rest of the world in terms of the speed at which change occurs. This means that many of the marketing and advertising strategies I've discussed in this chapter will quickly become obsolete. In fact, in retrospect, some of them will appear so primitive that people will look back at them and laugh.

As a Web merchant, this means you have to remain vigilant, monitor changes as they occur, and quickly implement them as part of your marketing and advertising strategy. It's absolutely critical to your long-term success. If you don't, the whole thing will pass right by you.

Look for Trends

Marketing and advertising strategies on the Web promise to bring real excitement to this new marketplace. Interactivity, in particular, will allow Web marketers to provide services to their customers that can't be equaled in real-world businesses.

Pay attention to new developments. Read everything you can lay your hands on, and subscribe to publications that cover the online industry. Some are published in traditional paper format. Others are on the Web itself. And don't forget to look to your peers. Joining a discussion group that focuses on advertising and marketing on the Web is an excellent way to stay on top of things.

Monitor the Competition

Imitation is the sincerest form of flattery. Watch what your competitors are doing and learn from them. As I mentioned before, things will change quickly. Keeping up with the Joneses is a must in cyberspace.

EDUCATE YOURSELF

Become a student of the technology. It may seem a bit intimidating at first. That's only natural. But the more you know, the better prepared you'll be to make informed decisions in working with Web designers, your ISP staff, and other professionals.

WHAT'S NEXT?

The next step is to get ready for those orders that will come rolling in once your online business is up and running. Chapter 10 looks at the nuts and bolts of presenting your goods and services, processing orders, and getting your products out to your customers.

FOR MORE INFORMATION

Here are some magazines, e-zines (electronic magazines on the Web), and Websites that will help you learn more about online marketing and advertising and about the Web itself:

- ➡ *Wired* (*http://www.hotwired.com/wired*) *Wired* has emerged as the premier publication about the Internet and World Wide Web. Its design is as cutting edge as the Web itself and requires some getting used to. But it provides a wealth of information about the latest trends in cyberspace.
- ➡ *Internet World* (*http://www.iw.com*) *Internet World* is another excellent source of information and can be a good source of URLs.
- ➡ **e-zine-list** (*http://www.meer.net/johnl/e-zine-list*) This Website lists more than 1,300 online publications, some of which can be useful for finding marketing and advertising tips.
- ➡ **HotWired** (*http://www.hotwired.com/*) This e-zine is a spinoff of *Wired* magazine and an equally valuable resource.
- ➡ **Advertising Age** (*http://www.adage.com*) This online version of the ad industry bible newspaper focuses on advertising and marketing on the Web.

10

CUSTOMER SERVICE ON THE WEB

This gets us to the nuts and bolts of running your online venture. As with any business, it's all about customer service. It's about the appearance and user-friendliness of your Website. It's about the speed at which you fill orders and communicate with your customers. It's about finding customers and keeping customers.

WHAT ARE YOU SELLING?

Different products require different methods of selling and service. If you sell merchandise, your responsibility is to provide your customers with their merchandise as quickly as possible after it's ordered. You take orders over the Web, by fax, over the phone, or by snail mail. But it's delivered by the United States Postal Service or one of the other package delivery companies.

If you sell information, let's say from a subscription-only online newsletter, your product will be delivered electronically. Your responsibility is to provide the kind of information you promise with the frequency you promise.

If you're selling a service, then *you* are the product. If the service can be delivered electronically, you have the responsibility to deliver it in a timely manner and at the level of quality you've advertised. If you perform the service in person and use your Website as a way to drum up business, you need to show up when you say you'll show up.

PRESENTING YOUR OFFERINGS

For an online merchandiser, the presentation of merchandise must walk a fine line between beauty and practicality. There's nothing more pleasing to a marketer than a beautiful photograph or image of a product with some "I dare you not to buy me" copy. You see it all the time in magazines, in catalogs, and on television.

But when you try the same approach on the Web, you'll stumble over one very large problem—download time. In print and broadcast media, the entire offering jumps out at the viewer at once. On the Web, it arrives on the viewer's monitor in bits and pieces. And the more there is, the longer it takes to appear. If it takes too long, the customer will lose interest and head elsewhere. How long is too long? In my opinion, anything over fifteen seconds with a 14.4 kbps modem is too long. Customers with faster modems will see your pages that much quicker.

So you have a time constraint that will limit the number of photographs and images you can use on a page. This limitation requires real self-control on the part of many site designers. They can get so caught up in the overwhelming beauty and complexity of a page that they lose sight of the fact that it will take forever to download. This is an issue you should discuss with all your site design candidates when you're first inter-viewing them. It's wiser to spread your information over more pages than to risk losing customers by cramming a lot of infor-mation onto fewer pages.

THUMBNAIL GALLERIES

One way to offer your customers lots of images and still keep download times under control is to create thumbnail galleries. These are compressed (about 5k to 10k in size), low resolution mini-images. If a customer is interested in an item and wants a better look, he can click on the thumbnail to get a full-screen, high-resolution image. You can put the file size of the larger image next to its thumbnail so that customers will have some idea how long it will take the larger image to download.

LINKS

Links won't necessarily do anything to improve your bottom line, but they are a customer service that Web surfers have come to expect. Including them on your site can't help but win your customers' good favor.

TAKING ORDERS

You will have gone to a lot of trouble to create your Website—hiring a designer, finding an ISP and determining the features you need, planning the site, developing marketing and advertising strategies. You need to be equally attentive in creating an ordering system.

Why? Because this is how you get your money! When customers decide to make a purchase, you need to make it quick and easy. Otherwise they may change their minds.

The first step is to streamline the process as much as possible. This is another area where Web shopping can be made even easier than shopping over the phone with a toll-free number.

SHOPPING CARTS

If your customers enjoy letting their fingers do the walking when they buy with a credit card and a toll-free number, they'll love shopping carts even more.

A shopping cart allows your customer to select merchandise with the push of a button. As a customer moves through your site and views the different items you offer, each selection is accompanied by the price and a button that says "add to shopping cart." It's just like wheeling a cart through the aisles of a conventional store and tossing purchases in before hitting the checkout line.

When the customer is ready to complete the transaction, he hits a button that says "proceed to checkout." At that point he can review the items he's selected, the price for each, and the total amount of his order. He can also delete anything he decides he really doesn't want. When the order is ready, he enters his personal information and hits the ''submit order'' button to send the order on its way to your computer.

The process is even easier on subsequent trips. Because you'll have stored the customer's name and address, and his credit card number or another preferred method of payment, in your data base, he won't have to enter this information a second time. It's literally as easy as one, two, three—select the merchandise, proceed to checkout, submit order.

As I mentioned in the previous chapter, many shopping carts are created with cookies and won't function properly if a customer has instructed his computer not to accept cookies. Discuss this with your Website designer. If the designer is using a cookie to create your shopping cart, make sure this information is provided on your home page and on your order form.

GIVE YOUR CUSTOMERS CHOICES WHEN ORDERING

I touched on this earlier in the book. You can't expect that all your customers will send their orders over the Web. At the moment there's simply too much confusion and misinformation about the security issue. To make sure you don't lose their business, you'll need an 800 number and an order form that can be printed out and either mailed or faxed.

Remember, too, that people who don't have immediate access to the Web can still buy merchandise from you. Web pages can be printed out, just like any other document on the Internet. When they are, and they get circulated from one person to another, your Website has suddenly begun to function like a mail order catalog. If people see something they want to buy on the printouts, they need to know how to do it. This is one reason why your mailing address, fax number, and 800 number should be on every page of your site.

SEND A CONFIRMATION

The first thing you should do when you receive an order is send the customer a confirmation by e-mail. Let them know the order has been received and when to expect delivery. If there will be a delay because of an inventory shortage or other problems, include that information as well. The issue of how deliveries are handled by mail order businesses is strictly regulated by the Federal Trade Commission. It's certain to become an issue on the Web as well. We'll look at how the FTC handles this issue at the end of the chapter.

CREATING AN ORDER FORM

The order form is the most important page on your Website. After all, this is the page where your customers give you their money, which is the point of all this. It needs to be simple enough that they aren't turned off, yet thorough enough that the transaction can be completed efficiently. Creating your order form requires a great deal of thought and testing.

If you don't accept credit cards electronically, or your customers are uncomfortable sending their card information over the Web, your order form will have to be printed out and either faxed or mailed to you. It's a bit more work for your customers than ordering electronically would be, but it is completely secure. Of course, they also have the option of phoning in their orders to your toll-free number.

Fortunately, creating an interactive electronic order form and receiving encrypted credit card numbers is becoming easier and easier. (Isn't it wonderful how all these problems are solved so quickly when there's money to be made?)

At this point the critical issue is whether the software you use runs under the Common Gateway Interface. The CGI allows your customers to look up information in your data base, runs your shopping cart, verifies shipping information, and verifies credit card numbers instantly so your customers can receive an order confirmation while they're still online. If your operation is big enough to need it, the CGI can interface your order form with your inventory control system and make adjustments to your inventory as merchandise is ordered. It can even send order information to your accounting department.

Here's the information that should appear on an order form:

- Customer name, address, daytime and evening phone numbers, and e-mail address.

- Items being ordered, quantity and prices of each, total cost of the order, and any applicable taxes and shipping charges. This information can be compiled automatically by your shopping cart feature as each customer moves through your site.

- Preferred method of shipping. Give your customers a variety of choices. If they're anxious to receive the merchandise, give them the option of next day delivery via the USPS or one of the package delivery services. If they can wait and want to minimize their shipping costs, they'll be content with fourth-class snail mail.

- Preferred method of payment. Do customers prefer to use a credit card, a form of e-cash, or do they want to print out the form and send it along with a check or money order? Also indicate the currency that checks and money orders should be in with a statement that says: "Checks and money orders must be in U.S. dollars and drawn on a U.S. bank."

- Account number. If you open accounts for repeat customers, you'll need a place for them to enter their account number when they place an order. This is particularly important for business-to-business sites.

- Credit card number and expiration date.

- Order number. Include this with your order confirmation. This will give you and your customer a common reference point should a problem arise with the order.

SHIPPING YOUR ORDERS

As sophisticated as Web technology is becoming, no one has yet figured out how to send merchandise through cyberspace. For that task, you'll have to rely on the U.S. Postal Service or one of the package delivery services like UPS or Federal Express. Which you use depends on what you're shipping, how fast you want it to get to your customers, and how much you want to spend. Many of the big Web and mail order houses like L. L. Bean and Land's End have contractual relationships with one or more delivery services. Amazon.com, on the other hand, regularly uses the post office, as do many small businesses.

USING THE POSTAL SERVICE

It may be known as snail mail in cyberspace, but in fact the U.S. Postal Service has improved its service remarkably in recent years. Considering the sheer volume of stuff it has to move around the country, it really does a pretty darn good job. The USPS offers mail order businesses a wide variety of mailing services.

Express Mail

Express mail guarantees overnight delivery for letters and packages up to a certain size and weight. It's expensive but a great solution when a customer needs an item immediately.

Priority Mail

Priority mail offers expedited delivery of first-class mail when overnight delivery isn't necessary. Most priority mail is delivered in two days.

First-Class Mail

This is the standard method for delivering correspondence, bills, postcards, and other packages weighing less than eleven ounces. First-class mail weighing more than eleven ounces is automatically treated as priority mail.

Second-Class Mail

This is reserved for the publishers of newspapers, magazines, and other periodicals sold by subscription.

Third-Class Mail

Most commonly used by businesses and organizations that take advantage of bulk mail discounts that apply to mailings of 200 or more addressed pieces (usually printed matter) or fifty pounds or more of addressed pieces (usually packages or a mixture of printed matter and packages), third class includes advertising mailings, merchandise, and other materials weighing less than a pound. It excludes letters, bills, statements of account, and checks. These must be sent first class.

Third-class mail is what you would use for promotional literature if you decided to combine an online business with a mail order business, or when you promote your site through the mail. There are various requirements for bulk rate mailings, and an annual presort fee that must be paid to the post office where the mailings are made. Postage may be paid by permit imprints which are printed in the address area of the literature, provided a permit is on file with the post office where the mailings are made.

Fourth-Class Mail

This mail, which includes parcel post, is for packages, merchandise, and printed matter weighing more than a pound. Delivery can vary from two to seven days or more, depending on distance.

Business Reply Mail

This consists of preaddressed, prepaid postcards and envelopes that customers return through the mail. The sender of business reply mail only pays postage on the cards that are returned.

POSTAL BUSINESS CENTERS

The USPS maintains nearly a hundred postal business centers around the country to provide basic customer service to business mailers. Their services range from answering questions over the phone to providing assistance in designing a mail piece. Other services include:

- Establishing corporate accounts for Express Mail
- Information on mailing list management and services
- Mailing preparation
- Information on obtaining permits
- Obtaining mailing supplies (trays, sacks, Express and Priority mail envelopes and labels, stickers, rubber bands, etc.)
- Postal publications and next-step help

Should You Use a Shipping Service?

Sure, if its rates are cheaper than those of the USPS for the particular type of package you're shipping. And if you have a package that exceeds the size or weight limits of the post office, you'll have to use a shipping service. You should determine your shipping needs while you're getting your Web business organized. Compare the rates and delivery schedules of the post office to the various services. Also determine if there will be special situations in which a shipping service would be preferable to the post office.

Both UPS and Federal Express have Websites that do a good job of describing their services:

Federal Express (*http://www.fedex.com/*)
UPS (*http://www.ups.com/index.html*)

FOLLOW THE FTC MAIL ORDER RULE

So far, there are no rules governing the way online merchants handle the orders they receive. But I'm sure it won't be long before attention is drawn to this issue by disgruntled customers who have either had to wait forever to receive their merchandise or haven't received it at all.

When rules are put into effect, they're almost certain to be based on the Mail Order Rule created by the Federal Trade Commission in 1975 to address these same issues in the mail order industry. In fact, because there's really no difference between a mail order business and a Web business once merchandise has been ordered, the rule could apply almost exactly as written. It would just need a few minor adjustments to take into account the different methods of communication between merchant and customer that the Web allows.

Here's an overview of the rule. Because it's written for mail order merchants, I've added comments in parentheses that apply to Web businesses. As a businessperson dedicated to providing good service to your customers, you'd be wise to base your own order fulfillment system on the rule. For a complete copy of the Mail Order Rule, contact the Federal Trade Commission, Enforcement Division, Washington, D.C. 20580. Call 202-376-3475.

WHEN YOU PRINT OR MAIL A SOLICITATION (OR PRESENT MARKETING AND ADVERTISING INFORMATION ON YOUR WEBSITE OR IN ADS ELSEWHERE ON THE WEB):

The time period for shipping must be clearly and prominently stated in your solicitation.

You must have "reasonable basis" for expecting to ship the merchandise within the time period stated in your solicitation.

If you do not include a time period for shipping in your solicitation, you must deliver the merchandise within thirty days of receipt of the order. This only applies to orders that contain all the information needed for shipping and for which you have received complete payment.

IF THE ORIGINAL SHIPMENT DATE CANNOT BE MET:

You must provide the customer with a notice (via e-mail) giving him the option of canceling the order and receiving a full refund, or agreeing to a delay in shipment. This is commonly called a "delay" notice or "option" notice and must be sent as soon as you realize you cannot meet the deadline. It must include a revised time period in which the customer can expect shipment. It must also state that if the customer fails to respond, it means they're consenting to a delay of thirty days or less.

If you are unable to give a revised shipping date, the notice must state that fact. It also must state that the order will be automatically canceled unless (1) you ship the order within thirty days of the original shipping date and you haven't received a cancellation notice before shipment, or (2) you receive the customer's consent to the delay within thirty days of the original shipping date. You also must state that they have the ongoing right to cancel the order at any time.

IF THE REVISED SHIPMENT DATE CANNOT BE MET:

You must send the customer a second notice, called a "renewed option" notice, offering them the choice of agreeing to a further delay or to canceling the order and receiving a refund. In this case, however, they must respond in writing to agree to the delay. If you don't receive a response before the first delay period ends, you must cancel the order and send them a refund.

All notices must be sent by first-class mail (or via e-mail) and should include a prepaid postcard or business reply mail envelope for customers to send you their responses (on the Web they also can respond by e-mail). When you refund a customer's money, it must be sent by first-class mail. If the customer paid by cash, check, or money order, you must send the refund within seven days of the order cancellation. If the customer paid with a credit card, you must credit their account within one billing cycle after the order is canceled.

Remember:

It's extremely important that you keep careful records of all notices sent and all cancellations (which means you shouldn't delete e-mail messages to and from customers). These records are critical in protecting yourself if the FTC should investigate you. They're your only proof that you've complied with the rule. Without them, the FTC can conclude you've been doing business otherwise.

WHAT ARE THE PENALTIES?

There are any number of federal and state agencies whose ire can be aroused by mail order companies that stray off the beaten track. It's not unreasonable to anticipate Web entrepreneurs to attract their attention as well. In fact, there have already been convictions for Internet fraud and false advertising.

USPS inspectors are authorized to arrest people suspected of violations. The Federal Trade Commission can come after violators, as can the Food and Drug Administration and a number of state consumer fraud agencies. Violators can be charged with mail fraud, false advertising, and a host of other violations. Even the Better Business Bureau can get into the act by alerting the media to a business's unsavory activities. As regulations are tailored for the Web, there will no doubt be additional infractions identified.

WHAT CAN HAPPEN TO BUSINESS OWNERS FOUND GUILTY OF VIOLATIONS?

A variety of things, ranging from being driven out of business to being thrown in the slammer for a number of years and fined a lot of money.

The bottom line here is that engaging in illegal or unethical practices just isn't worth the effort, no matter where you conduct your business. To operate in this manner is unfair to your customers and could result in your prosecution.

WHAT'S NEXT

Throughout this book I've mentioned some of the practices that can be harmful—or even fatal—to your business. Chapter 11 takes a quick look at the most serious of these digital boo-boos.

11

PROBLEMS THAT CAN SINK
YOUR DIGITAL SHIP

The Web has been around just long enough to help people learn from the failure of others. As I mentioned in Chapter 2, it's a new frontier littered with the wreckage of many businesses that tried and failed to make a go of it. Here are some of the mistakes they made.

INSUFFICIENT PLANNING

For many businesses, the ability to do business on the Web has generated an almost hysterical rush to establish a presence in cyberspace. In their haste they fail to plan properly. They don't ask themselves why they want to be on the Web or what it will do for their business. They don't know whether the demographics of the Web are right for their company. They don't know if they have the right product or service. They don't know how they'll go about marketing. They don't create a business plan. What they end up with is a Website and no clue what to do next.

Creating a Web business requires the same careful planning and attention you would give a business in the real world. There's nothing magical about cyberspace. It's as risky a business environment—if not more so—as the real world. Sit down, ask yourself the questions posed in the early chapters of this book, and create a business plan. Otherwise you'll almost certainly fail.

HIRING THE WRONG DESIGNER

You must be extremely careful when you start looking around for a designer for your Website. There are a lot of people out there who consider themselves Web designers. Some are computer jocks who have mastered Web design technology. Others are graphic designers who have done the same. But even with the best of intentions, they won't be able to help you without the proper experience. Knowing how to do it and knowing how to do it right are two different things.

Web commerce is a new arena that requires new skills. Your designer needs to be experienced in creating sites for businesses similar to yours. The two of you need to be able to work collaboratively. She should be able to give you advice when you ask for it. She should also have an understanding of your needs and goals and the ability to defer her ego in the interest of helping you accomplish them.

That's not always the case. I've run into Web designers whose arrogance and "know-it-all" complexes make them impossible to work with. They develop a proprietary attitude toward their creations that results in an obsessive need to control everything. The practical business needs of the site can elude them altogether. This kind of designer must be avoided at all costs.

CHOOSING THE WRONG ISP

Not all Internet service providers offer the same services. This is why you must know exactly what you're going to need from an ISP before you start your search. When you begin to interview candidates to house your Website, you should be the one asking the questions. Don't go into the meetings expecting them to tell you what you need. If you don't know, how can they be expected to know? Refer back to Chapter 5 to review some of the questions you should ask.

GETTING OVERCHARGED BY ISPS
AND CONSULTANTS

There are as many charlatans in the Internet industry as in the rest of the world. Always get at least three quotes before you hire an ISP, designer, or other consultant. And don't always assume the person with the cheapest quote will do an adequate job. Ask for references and samples of previous work.

CREATING A BORING HOME PAGE

First impressions mean everything on the Web. Your home page is the gateway to your business. If it's boring, people will likely assume the rest of your site is also boring. You and your designer need to pay particular attention to its design. If it doesn't entice people to enter your business, it's not doing its job.

SLOW DOWNLOAD SPEEDS

Slow download speeds can be absolutely fatal to your business. Your customers simply won't wait around to see a page that takes too long to open, no matter how interesting it is. Keep your graphics small and don't use any more than are necessary. If you do decide you need a lot of graphics, use thumbnails. Remember the magic figure: fifteen seconds maximum loading time with a 14.4 kbps modem. Anything slower will do more harm than good, no matter how spectacular the page.

This gets back to the issue of choosing a Website designer. A designer familiar with business sites will know what you need and why you need it. A rookie designer will more than likely get carried away and want to make your site the electronic equivalent of a Barnum & Bailey sideshow. Remember, less is more.

LACK OF CONTENT

If you don't use all the tools at your disposal on your Website, you're doing yourself an enormous disservice. Interactivity, in particular, should be exploited to create a vital, exciting experience for your customers. Don't just have product and ordering information on your site. Host a chat room or discussion group related to your product or service. Have a Q&A page. Run promotions that get people involved. And don't forget those all-important links to other sites you think your customers will enjoy.

LETTING YOUR SITE STAGNATE

Web surfers expect change. With it, you generate repeat visitors, your site gets bookmarked, people create links to your business, and people tell each other about you. Without it, you become old hat real fast.

DIFFICULTY IN NAVIGATION

There's nothing more frustrating than getting lost on a Website. Yet I'm amazed at how often I find sites that seem to either take me in circles or cause me to smack my nose against a digital dead end, where my only option is to hit the back button to get back to the previous page.

Once again, this is a planning and design issue. Planning the structure of a Website is a daunting task, and the bigger the site is, the more complex the design process. I have a friend who designs Websites. Before she touches the keyboard, she creates—first on paper and then on her computer—a chart showing how all the pages on the site will relate to each other. You can look at the home page and see what pages visitors will be able to jump to from it. The same is true for all the other pages on the site.

By the time she's finished (which can be as long as a month if the site is big enough) she will have created what looks remarkably like an enormous family tree, with the home page the oldest generation in the family and all the other pages succeeding generations. The designs are quite remarkable to look at, and can take up as much as ten or twelve feet of paper pinned horizontally to the wall. Only when she's finished and has a thorough understanding of how people will get from one place to another does she begin work on the site.

INADEQUATE MARKETING

This is the old "If I build it, they will come" problem. But guess what: they won't. Because they won't know you're there. You have to tell them, and that requires all the promotional and marketing and advertising strategies I discuss in Chapters 8 and 9.

LAUNCHING YOUR SITE BEFORE IT'S READY

If you've spent any time wandering around the Web, you've no doubt run into the ubiquitous "site under construction" pages. Many have a picture of the kind of black and yellow barriers you might find at a real construction site, or a couple of guys wearing hard hats.

These things drive me crazy. My attitude is, if your site's not ready, don't put anything up on the Web. People seem to think that by announcing they're in the process of building a site, they're going to have a whole crowd of people holding their breath in anticipation until it's completed. But the reality is nobody cares. I don't know a single person who has ever bookmarked a site under construction because they wanted to be able to get back to it when it was finally up and running. So do your promotion and marketing in advance, but don't launch the site until it's finished.

That brings us to another problem. Make sure it *is* finished when you launch it. The "haste makes waste" syndrome certainly applies to people who put their businesses up on the Web before they've fine-tuned their sites. As a result, customers get lost on the sites, have trouble ordering merchandise, and encounter any number of other headaches. Most of them will never come back, and you'll look like an amateur.

POOR CUSTOMER SERVICE

The Web provides online merchants with everything they need to give their customers wonderful service. Yet you'd be amazed at how many businesses neglect to have an e-mail address or fail to include their phone number or fax number where people can easily find it.

There's absolutely no excuse for not having first-class customer service procedures in place from the day you first open for business. Ordering and paying for merchandise should be accomplished easily and quickly. Order acknowledgments should go out immediately, and any anticipated delays in delivery should be noted with an explanation. E-mail addresses, phone numbers, and other methods of contacting you should be prominently displayed on your site, and all communications from customers should be answered immediately.

Compared to all the other exercises you'll go through getting your site up and running, providing good customer service is easy. Don't ignore it.

BREAKING THE LAW

You can get into just as much trouble on the Web as in the rest of the world. Bad behavior online has resulted in convictions for fraud, libel, false advertising, obscenity, and other offenses.

One of the big issues is jurisdiction. Because the Web is essentially a borderless entity, some prosecutors are quite zealous in their pursuit of people from one state for breaking laws in other states. For example, a couple from California were tried and convicted on federal charges of obscenity in Memphis, Tennessee. They had never been to Memphis, but files from their computer ended up there when they were downloaded by a federal investigator to his computer. Now they're both doing several years in federal lockups.

Hopefully you won't be engaged in such activity. But be aware that there have been other precedents set in cases involving false advertising, copyright infringement, and fraud. These are three areas that online businesses must pay careful attention to. Don't get carried away with your advertising claims, make sure you use only original material on your site (or get permission to use material that's already copyrighted by others), and give your customers what they pay for when they pay for it. And don't be a spammer. First of all, it's obnoxious. Second of all, if you tie up an ISP's lines with a bunch of incoming or outgoing spam and it causes a disruption in their business, you can be sued for negligence.

INADEQUATE SECURITY

I saved this for last because (a) it's unlikely that anything will happen to you, but (b) if it does, you can be ruined overnight.

Protect your sensitive information by keeping it on a stand alone computer whose only connection is to the power outlet on the wall (or as hard copy in a filing cabinet). And remove information from your Web-connected computer as soon as possible after it arrives. Even though I continually grouse about how all the paranoia about Web piracy is overblown, it's really the attitudes of consumers I'm referring to. I'll admit that the safest approach for an online business is probably to assume the worst. A little fear will keep you on your toes. There's simply too much at stake to take chances.

WHAT'S NEXT?

When I first met Jim Spitznagel in 1996, his online venture was barely six months old. Now he's into his fourth year of operation, which makes him a grizzled veteran of cyberspace. In Chapter 12 we'll pay him a visit to see how the business is doing and what advice he'd give the fledgling Web entrepreneur.

12

A VISIT WITH A CYBERPIONEER

The first thing that strikes you about Jim Spitznagel is his demeanor. He's just a happy guy, the kind of fellow who would be successful running a storefront business (which he did for twenty years in Pittsburgh) that deals in a product he's passionate about (which he is about music).

As I mentioned in the introduction, meeting Jim in early 1996 provided the inspiration for this book. It gave me a glimpse of this wonderful new way of doing business and convinced me that it's the perfect environment for entrepreneurs with a good product, a willingness to work hard, and modest financial resources.

As I was finishing the book, I paid Jim a return visit to see how his business has fared and to pick his brain for tips on doing business in cyberspace. As you'll see, he's doing well. And he's still a happy guy.

So, it's been almost three years now. That makes you a veteran among entrepreneurs on the Web. How's it going?
It's going great, although I'll admit that there was a time about eight months ago when I was considering folding up shop. My other business [Level Green Recording Company] was really taking off, and Jim's had sort of hit a plateau. Business was steady but it wasn't growing at the rate I had anticipated.

That was September. But then in October the orders just started pouring in. I also started getting fifteen or twenty new subscriptions a day to the electronic newsletter I distribute from the Website, instead of the two or three I usually get. I couldn't figure out what was going on.

Then I found out from one of my new subscribers that *Stereophile* magazine had picked my Website to be on their list of editors' favorites. They published the list in the magazine and also put it on their Website. It was amazing. All the marketing I was trying to do on my own was just crawling along. Then all of a sudden this respected magazine puts me at the top of its list and things just go through the roof.

So press exposure is a great way to get attention?
Yeah. I'd been trying to get some press exposure for a long time. I'd sent out press releases. I'd called people. But I was just plugging along. Then all this happened just because one of *Stereophile*'s editors found my site and became a customer. So since then I've put any idea of giving up the business right out of my mind. It just keeps growing and growing. I've doubled the number of subscribers to my newsletter, to just over 2,500. In September I had around 1,200.

The site has really stayed the same since the last time we talked. Are you still with Spinners, the ISP in Cambridge, Massachusetts, that created your site? Are you still doing all the updates yourself?
I'm still with Spinners. I've had no problems at all. The company has been very easy to deal with. Any time I've had a problem, they've fixed it immediately. I'm also still updating all my inventory lists and prices. There's only one thing I can't change myself, a list of addresses that I need to maintain, and they make the changes as soon as I ask them to.

Do they give you counts of the number of visitors you've had to the site?
Oh, yeah. And I don't even have to ask for it. The first of every month I get the previous month's counts. They also have a Web page I can go to and see all the information on charts and graphs.

How many visitors are you getting each month?
The last time I checked, I was getting around 16,000. It's kind of like having a shop, with people walking by and stick-

ing their heads in to see what you have. Some people stay and buy stuff, and others say, "Nah. This isn't for me," and leave.

Can Spinners measure how far into the site people go?
They can, but I haven't really had time to look at it. They give me so much information, I would need a marketing director to spend a whole week straight just to analyze one month's worth.

Have you updated any equipment?
Nope. The only thing I reinvest in is inventory.

The last time we visited, you had been in business for about six months and had already gotten a lot of orders from overseas. Has that continued?
Yeah. I have regular customers in Germany and a few in Brazil. But we're shipping all over the world. For the first two years, more than 50 percent of our orders came from outside the United States. But that's changed in the last year, and I've learned that people in Europe and in Canada really watch the value of the dollar. I hear this from customers all the time. When their currency is strong against the dollar, business picks up.

Then there are other trends you can never figure out. Like in the last two months I've gotten a ton of orders from Maryland and Connecticut. I don't know what it is. They're from different towns and from people on different servers. The only thing I can figure out is that they're friends or people who work together and they're spreading the word. And I'll tell you something: word of mouth still gives you the most loyal customers.

Do you do a lot business-related purchasing on the Web? For instance, do you buy your supplies or your inventory online?
I do most of my ordering online. Most of my distributors have Websites, and those that don't have e-mail I can use to place orders. I make my initial contacts over the phone to establish a relationship. But after that I do almost everything online. The only thing I don't buy online are my mailing supplies, and I get those from the post office through their 800 number.

Let's talk about security for a minute. As you know, there are all sorts of fears about using credit cards to buy merchandise on the Web. What percentage of your customers order with credit cards?

It's easily 99 percent. And it's not a secure server and no one has ever complained. The 1 percent of customers who don't use their credit cards either call me up or send a fax.

I think there's a misconception generated by the media about the amount of paranoia that exists. Obviously my customers don't have a problem. And of the 1 percent or so who call me up, a lot do it just to make the personal contact. It's like me calling up my distributors when I first started ordering from them. I think giving me their credit card number over the phone is their excuse to make personal contact, and that's fine with me.

Do you have a second computer that's not connected to the Web to keep confidential information on?

No. I keep all the credit card numbers on hard copy in a file. The way our shopping basket works is the customers set up a registration that includes their address and credit card information. I get that on e-mail. I take it off the e-mail, print out the information on hard copy, and put it in the file. So the only information that's left on the computer is their ordering information.

Have you looked at any of the electronic cash systems that are available?

I looked at one and I didn't understand it. And I did have one customer who refused to buy from me because I don't use it. But it's not that I won't use it, I just don't have time to study it.

Has your computer ever been broken into?

No. But if someone did break in, I don't know what information they would want. I suppose if someone was mischievous and just wanted to mess up my site, they could. But I think that's unlikely. I just don't have the kind of business that's politically correct or incorrect.

Have you had any problems with credit cards?

Just little ones, like customers getting their card numbers wrong, missing digits or getting them out of sequence, that sort of thing. Very early on there seemed to be some people trying to rip me off with phony numbers and phony addresses. But that completely stopped after the first few months.

I always get a verification number for all orders, no matter how small. And I'll compare addresses if I'm suspicious. I've been in business long enough that I sort of have a sixth sense that sends up a red flag if an address doesn't sound right.

How do you get the credit card transactions taken care of?
I still have all the charges transferred electronically to my bank at the end of the day. They take out their charges and credit my account with the balance. It's so easy. I have no paperwork, although if I want it I can print it out. My bank gave me the program for free and came to my office to install it. And there are no additional charges. The program is called Personal Ticket Capture, Version 2.5. It's made by a company called First Data Resources.

You mentioned earlier having tried different marketing strategies. What have you done?
I'm registered with all the search engines, and I'll reregister every few months so my site will appear closer to the top when people do searches. But that's really time consuming.

I also did nonflame postings to newsgroups. I would go to a specific site, let's say one that was about jazz. I would include a heading that said "CDs for Sale/Advertisement." Then the message would say "Jazz CDs for Sale. $8.00. Check out this Website." And then I'd include my URL. I'd keep it very specific and very short and simple. People could see from the heading that it was an ad and they could ignore it if they chose to. I did it for months and the only complaint I got was that I didn't include enough information. The person wanted the inventory and shipping information and didn't want to look up the Website.

That made me realize that there are some people on newsgroups who don't want to deal with the Web. They just want to deal with the newsgroups. To them, that's what it's all about. Some people just want e-mail and they don't want to know anything else.

I'll also look at the WTBs, the "want to buy" ads that you can find on all the music sites. People who are looking for certain recordings will put up postings announcing what they're looking for. I try to spend an hour a week going through these to see if there's anything that I have in stock. There always is.

Have you done any link exchanging, linking your site to other sites in return for them creating links to you?
I don't have any links on Jim's Ithaca Music Shop. It kind of goes back to my days when I had a regular retail store. You learn that you have to be careful who you associate with. I figured this whole thing is too new. I've had people approach me with proposals to do cross links, but I don't know who these people are or how legitimate they are. I wonder how many of them are still in business. Three years ago there were a lot of sites that don't exist anymore.

For my other business, Level Green Recording Company, I do have a few links. But they're mostly musicians who have their own Web pages.

How about cyber malls? Have you looked into them?
Yeah, but I don't like them, either. They're so big, I find them kind of overwhelming. Myself, I don't find things any faster using those malls. I think it's just as easy to find things doing a Web search. I think malls are a neat idea, but I don't think they're done right yet.

Are you still processing your own orders and shipping the same way?
Yes. I keep everything we list on the Website and in the newsletters in our inventory right here. As soon as I get an order, I process it and get it boxed and ready to go. At the end of the day I load them all up and take them to the post office. Everything I ship in the United States I send Priority mail. You can ship up to six CDs for three bucks and it's two-day delivery. Customers love it. There's very seldom a problem, and if there is, I just give them a refund immediately, no questions asked. If an order hasn't shown up in two weeks, it's not going to show up.

So you just eat the sale?

Yeah. It's worth it to keep the customer happy and to earn repeat business. Why have an unhappy customer? Especially on the Web. Who knows if the customer might flame all the newsgroups and say terrible things about you? I see that stuff all the time.

What's been your biggest order?

I won't give you an exact figure but it was for several hundred dollars from a regular customer in Europe who's actually a retailer. I have a lot of cutouts and things that are out of print and they're really hard to get over there. So I charge him my normal price and I know he's marking them up and selling them for a profit. He's probably doubling or even tripling his money, and more power to him. To save shipping costs, we take all the CDs out of their cases and stack them between sheets of fabric when we ship them.

How has overall sales growth been?

In the first six months I pretty much paid for my startup costs, which were around $20,000. The rest of that first year sales basically stayed flat. Then in the second year, I doubled sales, but by the end of the year sales were flat again. But then in the third year, sales doubled again. So basically I've had a hundred percent increase in sales each year. I realize it sounds great, but the actual figures aren't all that big yet. But it keeps growing, so it's worth doing.

But at least you're making money. And that makes me wonder if the Web isn't a better business environment—at least at the moment—for small businesses like yours, with little investment required, than for huge businesses like Amazon.com., which require enormous amounts of capital. That company has seen steadily increasing revenues since it started, but it's still not making much money.

I think the Web is the best small business environment. There's no doubt about it. You don't need a lot of capital, and if you're crunched for time with family or even a part-time job, it's perfect. In the real world, you can't have a business and not have regular store hours, seven days a week.

On the Web you're open all the time, and you work it around your schedule. There's no other job or business like that.

But you still have to provide good customer service.
Sure, although it's getting harder to do as I get busier. I'll get an e-mail from England wanting to know what shipping charges will be. It's hard to get right to it sometimes and things might slip through the cracks until I suddenly realize two days later that I haven't sent a reply.

What do you do when you go on vacation?
I take my laptop and check my e-mail constantly. I can't ship orders but I can send customers a reply. I'll say, "I'm on vacation, I'm having a great time, and I'll ship your order as soon as I get back." No one has ever gotten upset with this. In fact, people have written back saying, "Take your time. Have a good vacation," or "Where are you? What's it like there?"

But the funniest one was when I was in Portland, Maine, and told a customer I was there on vacation and he wrote back that he lives in Portland, Maine. If I had known, I could've brought his order with me and delivered it to him.

Do you spend a lot of time keeping up with the technology?
No, not nearly as much as I should. Something will suffer. I need to concentrate on the business side of things. I do try to sort things out, and of all the things that come across my desk each month, I might find one thing I need to pay attention to. But my basic attitude is, "When I need it, I'll learn it."

The only technology I worry about is having a better computer. But as far as the site itself, I think I was fortunate that Spinners is so good. I insisted that the site be kept simple, and they designed it that way. I still get lots of compliments on how easy the site is to use.

Do you look at other sites for ideas or to keep up with the competition?
No, I really just look at other sites for amusement. As far as competition goes, when I had my retail store, my philosophy was that my toughest competitor was me. If I did something

good one day, I'd try to do it better the next. If I did something bad one day, I'd never do it again. I just didn't worry about what other retailers were doing. I knew my business and I concentrated on it and tried to make it better. It's the same thing here.

Most of the music shops on the Web are like giant chain stores. I'm a specialty shop, that little corner of the Web where you can get hard-to-find blues and jazz and other music. When you come to me you're getting knowledge, personal service, fast service, and good prices. The chain stores can't do that.

So what has been your best marketing tool?

Without question, it's been the newsletter. I don't include everything I stock in it, but I'll highlight what's new or something that I'm recommending. I also write reviews of recordings. Everyone who subscribes receives the newsletter via e-mail every two weeks. I write it, edit it, convert it to a text file, and hit just one button, and it goes to every subscriber. Right now there are more than 2,500 subscribers and it's growing daily.

I tried sending this out on different days to test it, and I've found that Sunday morning is the best time. Within an hour of sending it, I can be sold out of items that I promote in the newsletter. The orders come in on Sunday, I package them up on Sunday night, and the first thing Monday morning they're all out. Then the people who get the newsletter at their offices get to work on Monday morning and a whole new rush of orders comes in. And they trickle in all during the week. It's remarkable how much business it generates.

One last question. What are the three most important pieces of advice you would give to people who want to start a small business on the Web?

Assuming they already have a product, the first piece of advice would be to shop around to find a service provider and a site designer. Ask tons of questions, and don't pay more money than you have to. Don't pay thousands of dollars to get your site designed. Pay hundreds of dollars. I know a lot of people who really got ripped off by their designers. There are real horror stories.

There are a ton of people designing sites for reasonable prices. Keep it simple, find someone who specializes in small businesses, and find out what they charge. Also, you can find sites you like and see if the designer's name and e-mail address are on it. Another good tip is to deal with someone local so you can look over their shoulder and work on the site together.

Here's an example. The site for my other business, Level Green Recording, is very, very simple. It doesn't have a shopping basket or any of that. It's pretty much an information site. I hired a guy to set it up. It has three pages of information. Two pages have photos, information, and links. The third page is all links to different sites. I paid $200 to have the whole thing set up.

The second piece of advice would be to find a bank that has the same credit card program that I have. Everyone I've ever talked to says this is the greatest thing in the world. And keep going through different banks until you find someone who offers it, because not all banks do offer it.

The third piece of advice would be to make sure that they're committed to providing good customer service, and that means answering e-mail. I say this because I've noticed that people think they're going to start a Web business while they have another job, the orders are going to come in, and they're going to come home from work and fill those orders and it's that easy.

But it's not. It's just like dealing with customers in the real world. If customers on the Web aren't provided with the information they want from a certain site, they'll go somewhere else. It's more than an hour a day. It's not something you check while your kid is taking a nap. You have to run the business, and you have to run it every day.

Would you do it again?
No question about it. I'd do it all over again. My only complaint is that I'd get a lot more computer for my money if I did it now than I did three years ago.

13

SITES YOU CAN LEARN FROM

This book has taken you step by step through the procedures needed to start a business on the World Wide Web. Here are sixteen sites you might want to visit to get an idea of how various companies have set up their own electronic storefronts. Some of the businesses are quite large, and others, including Jim Spitznagel's compact disc business, are run by just a few people.

The sites themselves illustrate a variety of sophistication. Some are relatively simple and inexpensive to create. Others required tens of thousands of dollars. Chances are you'll be able to find a business that's similar in size or focus to yours.

As you visit these sites, be aware of how you respond to them as a consumer. Do the graphics appeal to you or does the site look barren? Is it easy to find what you're looking for? Are there things you'd do differently? Are there features or services you think are missing? Keep in mind that Website design is rapidly changing. It won't be long before video and audio will be as commonly used as photographs and graphics. In two years what we see today will seem like ancient history.

Pay particular attention to how each business handles its ordering procedures, what kind of customer service information it includes on its site, and how it deals with credit cards and other security issues. No matter how much life on the Web changes in the coming years, these three issues will always be paramount to the success of all online businesses.

AMAZON.COM
(http://www.amazon.com)

Although it's certainly not the kind of site the average small businessperson would create on the Web, all cyberentrepreneurs should regularly visit Amazon.com to keep up on the latest in Website technology. With enormous financial resources and technological expertise behind it, this site will be one of the standard-bearers for new ideas in doing business on the Web.

JIM'S ITHACA MUSIC SHOP
(http://www.jims.com/)

Jim Spitznagel's compact disc business in Ithaca, New York, continues to be an excellent example of how a one-person, home-based business can thrive on the Web. His modest site is well-designed and well-thought-out and easy to navigate. It's also simple enough that he can update it himself.

Jim has another site for a new business venture, Level Green Recording Company *(http://www.levelgreen.com/)* that he's also operating out of his home. Level Green is his first foray into record production. The site has information and an order form for the company's first two releases.

TRAXX GOLF
(http://www.traxxgolf.com)

To say that golf is big on the Web is an understatement. Traxx Golf is a Dallas-based company that sells what it claims is the best new putter design to hit the market in more than twenty-five years. The company's Website gives an extremely detailed description of the putter's design and the theory behind it as well as testimonials from happy users. A well-designed order form gives customers the option of ordering over the Web or by fax.

The site also has a dozen or so links to other golf-related sites. Chances are that the owners of Traxx and the owners of the other sites have all agreed to link to one another. It's a good strategy for drumming up business that won't cost you a penny.

INDIAN HARVEST
(http://www.indianharvest.com)

Indian Harvest in Bemidji, Minnesota, built its business over the past twenty years supplying specialty rice, grains, and beans to some of America's most well-known chefs. The company now markets its products to consumers around the world. They work closely with growers to produce quality ingredients and then process them in a state-of-the-art facility in northern California. Many are quite rare to the market and have never been grown commercially before.

The company's Website is well-organized and easy to use. It offers the shopping basket feature and is set up for both domestic and international orders.

THOMPSON CIGAR COMPANY
(http://www.thompson-cigar.com/)

If you're a cigar smoker, this site will get bookmarked real quickly. Thompson & Co. is a Tampa, Florida, firm that's been in the business since 1915. The company also sells pipes and pipe tobacco and a large selection of cigar accessories.

This site's lack of sophistication is certainly made up for by its selection. Thompson sells approximately 200 brands from around the world. The site includes extensive descriptions of each brand, including country of origin and fascinating anecdotes about the manufacturers. You can even buy cigars made with tobacco grown in an extinct volcano in the Canary Islands.

SHRIMP.COM
(http://www.shrimp.com)

This is what Forrest Gump would have probably ended up doing if the movie had been a little longer. Shrimp.com in Aransas

Pass, Texas, markets shrimp to "the customer wanting high-quality seafood, with high-quality service." The company catches its product in the Gulf of Mexico, processes it at its Corpus Christi plant, and sells it in prepackaged five-pound units. The shrimp are quick-frozen upon receipt of each order to ensure a "boat fresh" presentation upon delivery.

Shrimp.com's modest but attractively designed Website has prices for three sizes of shrimp and Federal Express charts so customers can calculate their own shipping costs. It also has a page of photographs of its products and a recipe page with instructions for preparing several dozen very tantalizing shrimp dishes.

PETALS
(http://www.petals.com)

This White Plains, New York, company has been in the silk flower business for more than sixty-five years. They have a wide array of flowering plants, arrangements, green plants, and other products—all made from silk.

The Petals Website is well-organized, although not particularly attractive. There is a shopping basket option and an e-mail address customers can use to ask questions about home or office decorating.

A. G. RUSSELL KNIVES, INC.
(http://www.agrussell.com)

A. G. Russell is a big name in sporting knives. The Springdale, Arkansas, native started the nation's first "knives by mail" company in 1964. As recently as 1988 the company had only three employees. Today it has around twenty to handle its rapidly growing business.

This is a particularly well-designed site. It includes a variety of both production knives and handmade knives, as well as an area with used knives, including collector-quality items. It has the shopping cart feature and an easy-to-use ordering system.

GARDENER'S SUPPLY COMPANY
(http://www.gardeners.com/)

Gardener's Supply Company was founded in Burlington, Vermont, in 1983. Its catalog business reaches millions of gardeners throughout the United States and offers everything from seeds to greenhouses.

The company was among the first wave of businesses to expand to the Web. Its site was recently redesigned and expanded to allow the addition of hundreds of new products. It features a Gardening Q&A service that allows customers to get advice from staff horticulturists, as well as links to other interesting gardening sites.

JOHNSTON & MURPHY
(http://www.johnstonmurphy.com)

Johnston & Murphy is one of the country's oldest and finest men's footwear companies. They've been in business in Nashville, Tennessee, since 1850. The company's Website offers a comprehensive selection of dress and casual shoes, belts, socks, ties, and leather goods. It's well-thought-out and easy to use. There are sale items, special services, frequently asked questions, and a list of all the company's retail outlets. Each style of shoe is illustrated with a photograph, and a scroll bar allows customers to select sizes.

If, like many people, you have a deep-seated hatred of shopping, the ability to buy quality shoes and apparel from a company like this while sitting at your computer is a blessing. For companies selling clothing and footwear online, the future is bright indeed.

VIRTUAL VINEYARDS
(http://www.virtualvin.com/)

Virtual Vineyards is one of the oldest and best known sites on the Web. It opened for business on January 1, 1995, and offers an enormous selection of wines, gourmet foods, cookware, cookbooks, and other merchandise. The site is a good example of how your site can offer your customers a great deal more than just products. There's information on wine-tasting, e-mail links to food and wine experts that customers can use to pose questions, recipes and recommended wines to accompany each dish, and much more. It's a site that any lover of wine and gourmet cooking can spend hours in.

SKIN LIFE ONLINE
(http://www.skinlife.com/)

Skin Life Online is the creation of Jon Morgan, a dermatologist in Columbia, South Carolina, and an assistant clinical professor of dermatology at the University of South Carolina School of Medicine. The company markets a wide line of custom skin care products under Morgan's name. They include cleansers, toners, moisturizers, sunscreens, hair and body care products, and antiaging creams.

SPORTS WAREHOUSE
(http://www.sportswarehouse.com/)

Sports Warehouse is a Virginia-based company created specifically for the Web in 1995. The company offers a wide range of equipment for football, baseball, hockey, basketball, soccer, volleyball, softball, and the martial arts. The site is very well-designed and provides particularly good information about ordering and security.

eTOYS
(http://www.etoys.com)

Another of the larger Web merchants, eToys is an online toy store based in Santa Monica, California. The company carries toys from most major manufacturers, including Hasbro, Mattel,

Fisher-Price, and Brio. It also carries children's software and books. The site offers top-of-the-line customer service, an easy ordering procedure, and excellent security.

BLOSSOM FLOWER SHOPS
(http://www.blossomflwr.com/)

Blossom Flower Shops were founded in the Bronx, New York, in 1925. The company was one of the first floral businesses in the country to go online. It offers full-service floral services, including FTD, and accepts international orders.

ETHEL M CHOCOLATES
(http://www.ethelm.com/)

This site will get your mouth watering. Ethel M Chocolates is a rapidly growing business based in Henderson, Nevada, just outside Las Vegas. The company has nine retail shops in Las Vegas, including several at the Las Vegas airport, and is expanding into other parts of the country, including other airports. The company's nicely designed Website offers a broad selection of chocolates. It uses a shopping cart feature and is very easy to navigate.

GLOSSARY OF INTERNET AND
WORLD WIDE WEB TERMS

@   This character, prounounced "at," separates a userid and the domain name in an Internet address.

ASCII   A basic text format that can be read by most computers. The acronym stands for American Standard Code for Information Interchange.

attachment   A file sent along with an e-mail document.

bandwidth   The data capacity of a transmission line.

bit   The smallest unit of binary data.

bits per second (bps)   The rate at which data can be transferred between two modems. The greater the bps, the faster data can be sent.

bookmark   A URL stored in a file by a Web browser for quick access. Most Web users will bookmark their favorite Websites.

bounced message   An e-mail message that's returned to the sender. The usual problem is an error in the address.

browser   A software program used to retrieve HTML documents (Web pages) and then display them on a monitor.

byte   The equivalent of one text character. A byte consists of eight bits.

cache   A temporary file storage. For example, a Web browser will cache the files it downloads from Websites.

chat   A real-time, online discussion group.

CERN   The physics laboratory near Geneva, Switzerland, that was the birthplace of the World Wide Web.

click stream   A sequence of URLs clicked by a Web user.

click-stream analysis   A report of the URLs visited in a click stream.

click-through   A Web advertising term referring to a user clicking on an online advertisement.

commercial service   A generic term for online services such as America Online and Prodigy.

compression   The shrinkage of computer files to save storage space and reduce transfer times. There are special utility programs to perform this task available for most computers.

cracker   A person who breaks into a computer system to steal files or disrupt activity; an electronic vandal.

dial-up access   A computer connection made over standard telephone lines.

domain name   The word in an Internet address that identifies the "location" of the user. For example, in the address *Walt @Disney.com*, the word "Disney" is the domain name.

e-mail   A short term for "electronic mail."

e-zine   A magazine published solely in electronic form and accessible over the Web.

FAQ   "Frequently asked questions." Usually a list of answers to questions most often submitted by visitors to a Website.

flame   An unusually derogatory and malicious response to another person in a newsgroup or message area. Usually sent in response to a breach of netiquette.

flame war   A back and forth series of flames.

file transfer   The transfer of a file from one computer to another over a network.

frames   A style of Web page layout that allows two or more pages to be viewed at the same time.

Free-Net   A commuity-based network providing free Web access to local residents.

freeware   Free software that can be downloaded from the Web.

FTP   File Transfer Protocol, the standard protocol used to transfer files from one computer to another.

GIF   Graphics Interchange Format, a common file format for images.

gopher   A guide to directories on the Internet organized in a menu format.

hacker   A person who enjoys exploring computer systems and is often challenged by entering secure systems. Unlike a cracker, a hacker is not malicious, just nosy.

hit   A request to a Web server for a single file.

home page   The first page users encounter upon visiting a Website.

host   A server computer that houses software and provides services to other computers connected to the Web.

HTML   Hypertext Markup Language, the universal language of the Web. HTML coding is used to format Web pages and create hypertext, the links that allow users to point and click their way from one site to another.

http   Hypertext transfer protocol, the technical standard for delivering Web pages to Web browsers.

hypertext   The text used for the links that allow users to point and click their way around the Web. The text usually appears in blue and is underlined and then turns to red or purple after it's been clicked.

IETF Internet Engineering Task Force, the group that recommends and reviews technical specifications and standards for the Internet.

Internet The global network of interconnected computer systems.

Intranet A private network created using the standard Internet protocols.

IP Internet Protocol, a set of standards that determine how information is transmitted on the Internet.

ISDN Integrated Services Digital Network, the set of standards that govern transmission of data over standard telephone lines.

ISP Internet Service Provider, a business that provides Internet access to individuals and businesses.

Java A programming language that can be used with Internet applications. It was developed by Sun Microsystems.

JPEG Joint Photographics Expert Group, a graphics format that compresses data.

kbps Kilobytes per second, a term used to describe the transmission speed of modems and other transmission devices.

kilobyte One thousand bytes of data.

LAN Local Area Network.

lurker A person who logs on to usegroups to read messages but who never joins in the conversations.

megabyte One million bytes (1,000 kilobytes) of data.

MIDI Musical Instrument Digital Interface, computer-created synthesized sound.

MIME Multipurpose Internet Mail Extension, a protocol that allows files to maintain their formatting when sent as attachments to e-mail.

modem   A device that allows computer users to access the Internet over conventional phone lines. It modulates the signal between digital and analog.

MPEG   Motion Pictures Experts Group, a file compression format used for audio, video, and a combination of both.

Netiquette   The unwritten rules governing communication behavior on the Internet.

newbie   A person who is a newcomer to the Web.

Newsgroup   A Usenet discussion group.

OPS   Open Profile Standard, a proposed technology standard for sharing personal information over the Internet.

P3   Platform for Privacy Preferences, a technique being developed that will allow users to find out what personal information is being collected when they visit a Website.

packet   A chunk of data that's transmitted over the Internet. A packet is usually about 1,500 bytes.

page   See Web page.

POP   Post Office Protocol, a methodology used to get e-mail.

posting   Sending a message to a public message area.

protocol   The techniques used to create a method of communication between computer hardware and software.

server   A computer (and software) that acts as a host for various resources, including Websites.

SET   Secure Electronic Transaction, a standard developed for the secure transmission of credit card information over the Web.

SLIP   Serial Line Internet Protocol, the direct connection between a computer and the Internet.

SMTP   Simple Mail Transfer Protocol, the most commonly used method to exchange e-mail between servers.

snail mail   Mail delivered by the U.S. Postal Service.

spam The mass sending of e-mail to as many newsgroup members as possible. A particularly unpopular form of electronic advertising.

T-1 The smallest fiber-optic cable. A T-1 can support transmission speeds up to 1.54 mbps.

T-3 A larger fiber-optic line with the capacity of 28 T-1 lines. Supports transmission speeds up to 45 mbps.

Telnet A process that allows a computer to be controlled from a remote location.

thread A posted newsgroup message and all the subsequent replies.

URL Uniform Resource Locator, or put more simply, a Web address.

userid The name given to a user on a system for e-mail. For example, in the address *Walt@Disney.com*, the word "Walt" is the userid.

WAN Wide Area Network.

Web page A single HTML document as it appears in a user's browser (and also on the user's monitor).

Website A collection of HTML documents stored on a computer, that can be viewed from remote locations.

Web server A computer and software that deliver HTML documents or files to Web users upon request. A server is the host of a Website.

WWW The World Wide Web.

World Wide Web Consortium (W3C) An international consortium organized in 1994 to develop common protocols for the development of the Web.

INDEX